LEONARD DIEPEVEEN

WHEN I COME BACK WE WILL TALK

My Father, the War, and Me

Freehand Books gratefully acknowledges the financial support for its publishing program provided by the Canada Council for the Arts and the Alberta Media Fund, and by the Government of Canada through the Canada Book Fund.

This book is available in print and Global Certified Accessible™ EPUB formats.

Freehand Books is located in Moh'kinsstis, Calgary, Alberta, within Treaty 7 territory and Métis Nation of Alberta districts 5 and 6, on the traditional territories of the Siksika, the Kainai, and the Piikani, as well as the Iyarhe Nakoda and Tsuut'ina nations.

Thanks to Faber and Faber Ltd. for permission to quote an extract from Sylvia Plath's "Lady Lazarus."

LIBRARY AND ARCHIVES CANADA CATALOGUING IN PUBLICATION
Title: When I come back we will talk : my father, the war, and me / Leonard Diepeveen.
Names: Diepeveen, Leonard, 1959- author
Identifiers: Canadiana (print) 20260216682 | Canadiana (ebook) 20260216771 | ISBN 9781997534303 (softcover) | ISBN 9781997534327 (PDF) | ISBN 9781997534310 (EPUB)
Subjects: LCSH: Diepeveen, Leonard, 1959-—Family. | LCSH: Amersfoort (Concentration camp) | LCSH: Holocaust survivors—Netherlands—Biography. | LCSH: Children of Holocaust survivors—Canada—Biography. | LCSH: Holocaust survivors—Psychology. | LCSH: World War, 1939-1945. | LCSH: Jewish families—Canada. | LCGFT: Biographies.
Classification: LCC FC106.J5 D54 2026 | DDC 940.53/18092271—dc23

Edited by Deborah Willis
Design by Natalie Olsen
Author photo by Angie Morash
Paddleboat photo by John Bron
Psalmboek photo by Theo Legters
Printed and bound in Canada
FIRST PRINTING

FREEHAND BOOKS
freehand-books.com

Canada | Canada Council for the Arts | Conseil des Arts du Canada | Alberta Government
CERTIFIED CANADIAN PUBLISHER

MIX
Paper
FSC
www.fsc.org
FSC® C100212

For Dirk Diepeveen, at Rest

CONTENTS

There is a charge

For the eyeing of my scars, there is a charge
For the hearing of my heart —
It really goes.

And there is a charge, a very large charge
For a word or a touch
Or a bit of blood

Or a piece of my hair or my clothes.

— Sylvia Plath, "Lady Lazarus"

Finally, brethren, whatsoever things are true, whatsoever things are honest, whatsoever things are just, whatsoever things are pure, whatsoever things are lovely, whatsoever things are of good report; if there be any virtue, and if there be any praise, think on these things.

— Philippians 4:8

Prologue

MY FATHER DIED on December 22, 2023, in his ninety-sixth year. My calls to him over the last decade of his life had followed a single pattern: the phone rings and rings until he is able to shuffle over to wherever he had left it last. He is out of breath, and pants a while before he says "hello" in a weary yet curious voice, open towards whoever and whatever is on the other side of the line. His wavering "hello-o" uses three syllables now, his greeting a little more tentative and a lot more tired than it used to be. He has been radically slowing down. Even before answering he can probably guess it's me, or maybe my brother. We try to call every day, my brother from the next province over, and I from the other side of the continent.

"How was your day, Dad?"

"Oh, not *too* bad."

We have a comparative chat about the weather, the music he is listening to, or the puzzle he's been working on. He asks a question or two about my day. Sometimes he rouses himself to tell a dad joke. Occasionally he gets worked up about a few things: poverty, the state of the church, Trump ("This is how it begins, Len"). In its daily repetitions the call feels a little timeless, not that it takes much time. He always wants to close things off before I do. A lull in the conversation as his replies become shorter, he gives an open-ended "okay," and pauses, silent. He is done. Most days I get maybe three minutes.

But he says "I love you" at the end, without prompting. This is a new openness for him, poignant for its surfacing so late in life.

After the call he puts down the phone, and in my mind's eye I see him return to his jigsaw puzzle, bent over, become absorbed again, some soft music in the background, as he waits for the night. He is the classic old man, standing, alone, near the end of his life, looking at it somewhat resolutely, and ours is a conversation that so many others have also engaged in. A very long goodbye.

*

When I hugged my father in his final years, before leaving once again to board my overnight flight back to Halifax on the other side of Canada, I would enter into another kind of ritual, of touch and of the passage of time on his body, a ritual always the same. As I settled into our embrace, I would feel his scratchy cardigan with its old-man smell, stretched tight over the hump of his back, his shoulder blades now protruding, and his body curling into my chest as he hugged me. His tremor, in our tight contact, would be momentarily stilled. He had become much shorter than when I was a child, and it was not just the reversal of perspective, the son overtaking the father. Osteoporosis had so curved him that, when he stood, it took an effort for him to look someone in the eye. Eye contact became deliberate, and on this highly charged occasion, as always, we minimized it, fearful of where it might lead, to an uncontrollable eruption of grief and love. Now when we hugged I would look down on his wispy hair, the mottled skin thin beneath it, stretched close to the skull. "Thanks for coming," he would say, softly. And although he once again struggled to hold it off, when we settled into our physical contact he would begin to cry, looking away, as he always did. I would too.

It's a profound experience, deepened by its particularity, but not unique in its outlines. In North America, where the distances separating family members are often long, countless children of aged parents walk through some version of this – the long-distance plane trip that allows a short but intense visit, a visit which every time has the same emotional weight, of a hoped-for deep talk that doesn't happen, of noticing new frailties, of seeing off one's parent and watching them struggle as they move, slowly, to their end. But on these visits my father cried more than most – a lot more, and he shook constantly. In response, all I could rouse myself to do was offer inadequate comfort, and watch.

*

Sixty years earlier, my memory is not one of goodbyes, but of greetings. Before I had entered first grade, my life had a daily rhythm. The youngest child, I was home alone with my mother all day, playing with the white Volkswagen ambulance and the little hammer set my Dutch relatives had sent just for me. The ambulance, although it made a realistic siren sound when you pushed it, was a little disappointing because it didn't look like a Canadian ambulance, but the hammer set was fine – I can still see the box, "Hamertje Tik" printed on the front, above the silhouette of an industrious boy calmly working away on some indeterminate project. Then it was lunch (always sandwiches with either Gouda cheese or pungent, thinly-sliced *cervelat worst*, since for years my mother did not believe in Canadian peanut butter), followed either by visiting someone with my mother or playing some more. And then, late afternoon, I would wait for my father to come home from his work at the chemical plant. As he entered our back porch, I would fling myself from the top of four stairs, knowing he would catch me. He always did, without first setting down his black steel lunchbox, which would sometimes scrape me as I curved myself into his embrace.

This memory, scrubbed of its immigrant nuances, could stand in as the memory of many privileged children, growing up in safe homes – or perhaps of those misremembering their homes as safe. It suggests both a lucky story and a cliché from which any sharp edges have been sanded off. My father was strong; he was young, handsome, cheerful, optimistic, and I was completely safe, content, integrated. We were together; there was no silent gap pushing between him and me. This memory, too, feels like a timeless anecdote, a warm tableau of goodness and love. But of my scattered memories of my childhood, this is one of the few I have that in retrospect I feel was not surrounded by a vague penumbra of something unsettling and unsaid, created by a different tableau, of a man sitting alone at the head of a dinner table, a Bible open before him, the man looking not at it, but looking away, trembling and weeping.

KAMP AMERSFOORT

Winter, 1945

THE SHORT STORY is this:

> In the final months of the Second World War, when almost all of Europe had been liberated, during what was called the Hunger Winter in the still-occupied Netherlands, my father was arrested, interrogated for several days, and sent to a prison camp, where he was imprisoned for a month before being sent on to Germany. He barely survived. He was sixteen years old. He had another eighty years to live.

That is the short story. But, of course, things are more complicated than that.

*

I was a professor of literature for many years, working at a university in Halifax, Nova Scotia, on the eastern edge of North America, across the ocean from the Netherlands. In my teaching I was drawn to works about trauma, suffering, and loss – to the extent that, in one year-end evaluation, a student proposed that my introductory course be retitled "Death and Pestilence 1000." I guess you turn to things both that speak to you and that you think others should know, and don't examine too closely the apparent and natural equivalence of the two. So it was probably instinctive that as the son of a Dutch immigrant who had been brutalized by the Nazis I repeatedly turned, on my own and in my teaching, to *The Assault*, a novel by the great Dutch writer Harry Mulisch. The book follows the arc of its narrator's life, beginning with a short explosive event early in that life. In the final winter of the Second World War, with liberation happening across most of Europe but not yet in the Netherlands, members of the Dutch underground in Haarlem assassinate a Nazi police chief. They kill him near the home of narrator Anton Steenwijk (a boy about twelve years old) and his family, who are nothing more than bystanders. From behind their blackout curtains they don't even see the event; they just hear the gunshots. In a phrase that echoes throughout the novel, Anton and his family "had nothing to do" with the assassination, neither as heroes nor as collaborators. They were just there. Nevertheless, the Nazi retaliation is brutal, swift, and directed at those who just happened to be on the spot. That same night Anton's home is burned to the ground and his entire family is executed. In a moment, all is gone. But that horror covers just the first fifty-five pages of a much longer novel, which narrates discrete episodes from the decades that follow. Initially, one might think Mulisch has written himself into a corner. After this riveting beginning, a narrative in which the novel already seems to have reached its climax, how could Mulisch contrive to make the rest of the novel significant? How to account for the novel's bulk, and the likely disproportion of those following decades? How to avoid the pitfall of writing two hundred pages of denouement? Aware of this imbalance, and determined to make it sing, Mulisch sums up the rest of the novel and Anton's life in this way:

> All the rest is a postscript – the cloud of ash that rises into the stratosphere from the volcano, circles around the earth, and continues to rain down on all its continents for years.[1]

Trauma messes up cause and effect. Mulisch's sentence begins vaguely – the phrase "all the rest" speaks for everything but promises nothing. The rest of the novel, the rest of Anton's life, is a "postscript" – dependent, an eventless afterthought following the main event. And that afterthought, that cloud of ash, has a languorous quality, a desultory and unpredictable movement, but one that eventually, relentlessly, covers the whole world, raining down on continents. Escaping the falling ash is impossible. The grit coats the skin, gets in the eyes, into the lungs.

It gets in my eyes and lungs, too, falling from the same location and time as Mulisch's novel; and that which complicates a novel's narrative arc also creates difficulties and imbalances in a life. The short but brutal episode in 1945 defined and circumscribed the rest of my father's life – almost another eighty years – a life spent trying to keep his trauma at bay, to make a life for himself, despite everything. To be sure, it wasn't all ash for my father or his family. There were many good things over the years, but even so his life after the War functioned like a postscript, a response more than a lived event in which each day sets out on its own terms. This book describes the texture of that life, what happened and what it felt like afterwards – the experience of the War's ash settling and drifting, how my father and our family (my mother, older brother, two older sisters, and me, the youngest) breathed it in every day.

*

So, what happened during that winter of 1945? When I was a young boy, none of it was clear to me, although it was obvious something was up; before I heard my father's story I saw the event's effects in his behaviour and on his body. As to the causes of my father's behaviour, we children were all clueless, each of us for different lengths of time; I may have been clueless for the shortest. (Perhaps, in those years in the sixties and early seventies when the effects of his trauma took over our home life, I, as the youngest, spent more time watching, trying to catch on to the unstated patterns of home life.) In my early years I knew not much more than my father had been in a camp, and for some reason I knew what a camp was. But "he had been in a camp" is less a story than a state of being, a minimal, perhaps evasive reference to a condition at a specific moment in time. How I remember learning about my father's War is more like trying to recreate the texture of daily life than it is like narrating explosive events, more about living with it than learning about it. The context of how I came to know about individual details is diffuse, unlocatable. Except for a couple of moments in the mid-1980s and early 1990s, once when he wrote his one account of his War imprisonment (when I was in my early thirties), and another occasion a few years earlier (unwitnessed by me), the events of his War were revealed as a series of short, almost static anecdotes whose telling always was clipped, resisted follow-up, and unconnected except in a general way to other anecdotes. (Late in his life, he called these fragments the "gory details" – a term that was more a swipe at his sometime-listeners than a description of his own sense of things.) And the telling was always visceral, my father shaking, crying, looking away. From my childhood to his old age, when moments of his story surfaced, they were parcelled out, never in a single sweep, never with suspense, never with a climax or resolution, and so were all the more ominous for their sudden surfacing and disconnection from a larger context. My father didn't talk about his time in the prison camp so much as refer to it. There was no sitting down with a cup of tea at a kitchen table, talking things through over a couple of hours. Things came out unevenly, and I was given images whose embodiment and connections I had to imagine and fill in. To me, this was not unusual, and – perhaps as a result of my conditioning – I continue to think that this is the way we often come to know difficult things and experience our knowledge of them: we make a brief reference, acknowledge, deflect, and move on, until the next time. In novels it is different.

My father's story, disjointed as it was, was always there in front of me even when it was not being told; it was constantly pointed to, by my father's outbursts of uncontrolled sobbing, by his leaving the dinner table to go to another room, by his shaking, by his staring into a blank distance – or by my mother's resolute and grim silence in the face of all of that, by her refusal to comfort him in our presence, and by her pointing her children in a different, more practical direction. As opposed to those moments when bits of his story were revealed, this pointing to it was more difficult for me as a child than the story itself, because it gestured to what could not be expressed about what had happened, to what those fragments of the story could not contain, and to what could not be understood about my parents' differing relationships to his story, and to their lack of unity and peace with each other about it.

Fragmented as it was, then, the story of my father's War had a peculiar type of refracted control and rhythm, pivoting around two people, two opposing narrators and narrative controls: my father with his emotional excess, his weeping and shaking, his breaking down, and then his disappearances, his lying down by himself to tend to his headaches, his staring into a middle distance and a remembered past. And then my mother, with her parsimonious control over what we children would see and know of this War, with her shutting down of my father's crying, her closing off the explosive presence of the War during family devotions, her pursed lips and averted eyes from him and her children showing her shame and distaste for my father's weeping – not for his story, but for the excess and his lack of control, his inability to move on, to turn to other things, the way she did with stories from her own past. Her imprint on my father's living with his trauma includes her anger in his last years at her inability to shut things down, to stop his compulsive talking about the War, to keep everything under some semblance of control, and at his turning to a counsellor and not to her for a way to manage things. That, too, shaped his story.

As I learned of my father's War, piecing together anecdotes into the contours of a still-amorphous story, it became clear that the lack of connection among its parts was not a result of my being unable to organize the facts, my failure to capture the sweep of a narrative. The disconnection was simply a result both of what I had been given, and of how it had been given. My father's story was never going to be a tidy narrative, complete with characters clearly delineated and propelled by complex motivations, with a rich contextual background that settled his War firmly into history, with a rising and setting of action, and with, finally, some sense of closure. I was given a different kind of story, a disjunctive parcelling out that created its own kind of narrative, one of unbalanced proportions, of silences pushing back against revelations, of pressing and evasion, a narrative whose form and implications took me decades to understand, and then only imperfectly.

The form is its own kind of story, in which its disjunction and incompleteness revealed more profound things about my father than if he had been able to tell his story in one long, sinuous line. Yes, I came to know a few isolated things about the War, but the form in which I came to know those things created its own narrative, a narrative made up of both the War and the War's aftermath, both the eruption and the ash, a narrative whose two parts bounced and rattled against each other, unable to either be separated or cohere. In essence, five weeks in 1945 functioned as the antagonist in a larger plot, the plot of my father's remaining eighty years. The War entered the narrative of his later life the way it does in *The Assault*'s remaining two hundred pages: unannounced, abruptly, without his control, with a devastating emotional impact made worse by his inability to share it with his family. My father's life-narrative was messy and ungainly, but it was always one narrative, in which the War's aftermath, his remaining eighty years, was still, and always, the War.

The antagonist in my father's story has a name: from when I was a child it was always "the War" for me. The word was always capitalized in my mind, and always took the definite article. The War was a proper noun, a name, something like "Dad." "The War" wasn't just a name or a placeholder for a time period – it did things; it was an agent, even a character, in my father's story. But the War also took the definite article, which points in a second direction – after all, one doesn't refer to one's father as "the Dad," except ironically. *The* War is polemical. "The": for me as a child, and to some degree even now, there is no other war, only this one, always just the War.

Of course, there are and have been other violent conflicts that people call wars, but for me "the War" was not part of this larger category; it was *sui generis,* its own thing, by itself. In the context of his prison camp, in my family, it never was World War II. That may reveal some family myopia. But, given the War's decades-long grip on my father and our daily lives, our myopia seemed normal. The War was too close.

As for what happened during the War, I can pinpoint the few specific details that I came to know as a child – an arrest, a roll call, an escape after a train ride – but, until his last years, when my father spoke of the War more compulsively, I cannot recall specific moments in which my father told me something about his imprisonment. Until he began to speak specifically of the prison camp – Kamp Amersfoort – in his last two decades, the details about his imprisonment elicit for me no specific moment of telling; they were just part of the atmosphere of my growing up. What I do remember, clearly, is the experience of living with his story – of which the scattered details of 1945 were the painful origin, setting the terms and trajectory of our days together. Writing about how I remember living with and learning about my father's War has me reaching for the past continuous tense, that memory-sense of the atmosphere and character of ongoing, repeated past events which Marcel Proust, thinking about his own past and what it has added up to, invokes at the famous beginning of *In Search of Lost Time*: "For a long time I used to go to bed early. Sometimes, the candle barely out, my eyes closed so quickly that I did not have time to tell myself 'I'm falling asleep.'"[2] So, although I do not remember specific moments from my childhood in which episodes from my father's War were revealed to me, neither are my memories negligible – they just have a different quality and function from the remembered individual event. My childhood memories of my father's War are about the experience of living with it, and are situated in a recurring time whose events, despite their lack of temporal fixity, have a texture that is immediate, specific, forceful. When I think back, I relive the texture of ongoing events, events that were infused with the consequences of his War: dinner, church, family devotions. Their texture, then, is a kind of deflection, a standing in for something else from decades earlier that is both referred to and evaded, something ominous and malevolent. It seems a little incongruous: the temporally amorphous continuous past as a way of revealing and dealing with the specific time and events of explosive trauma. But that's the way it is.

Along the way I realized something that in retrospect is obvious: the act of writing about my father's War was pulling in a different direction from how I came to know his story. Beginning my work on this memoir in the year before he died had been an attempt to understand my father and a form of grieving for what was about to happen, for the shoe that was about to drop. But the act of writing about his War also allowed for some welcome distance, turning the events of 1945 – for moments, at least – into a problem of pacing, verb tense, sentence and paragraph structure, allowing me to think about his War and my life with him and it from a mediated distance, the pressure off, handling the material with white gloves on. Relieving me of the pressures of immediate presence, the mediation of writing made possible a linear chronological narrative, disentangling the War from the experience of living with the War. And so as I wrote, a bifurcation began to open up in his life story: there was the experience of his and my living with the effects of the War, and then there was the War, by itself, a single narrative, swift, brutal, and stark. Each had its own form and purposes of communicating. In the section that follows, that story of his life during the War, separated out as a linear narrative, has multiple sources: I have connected what I learned from my father to a larger public history of the War, and, eventually, to documents about my father from the time. Together, the different sources fill in silences and situate my father's War in a specific place at a specific time. With the following narrative of my father's War I move between the public and the private, and later in this book – once the historical War was done and needed to be lived with – into my family, and its own peculiar way of living with what had happened.

*

This is what I know to be true. It was winter, 1945. Most of Europe was free, but the Dutch corner of it was still controlled by an increasingly desperate Nazi regime and its collaborators. My father, and everyone in the urban west of the Netherlands, was starving. Suffering under a Nazi embargo on food shipments (in retaliation for a rail strike and Allied advances) people had been driven to eating tulip bulbs, cats, anything. In addition to the starvation it was brutally cold. It is called the Hunger Winter. In this setting, the Nazis had lowered the age of conscription from eighteen to sixteen and were aggressively rounding up every eligible male to send to Germany to aid in their disintegrating war effort. They needed bodies for hard labour, even emaciated bodies at the point of starvation. It was a difficult trade-off for the Dutch – help the Nazis or maybe starve to death and risk arrest and punishment for evading conscription. My father was living in Loosduinen, a suburb of The Hague. The oldest of four children, he was

My father, age sixteen, before Amersfoort

sixteen, and had already narrowly escaped a German press gang, hiding with other acquaintances and a German deserter in a barn, armed and prepared to die as the Nazis searched the area. In desperation, both over being unwilling to aid in the German war effort and to avoid starvation by remaining home, his parents decided to send him to live with his maternal grandparents in the village of Koekange in the province of Drenthe, in the rural East – closer to Germany, but where there was food, and where he could hide. The rest of the family would join him there later. But getting there, through the inevitable checkpoints, was fraught. His parents decided to falsify his identification papers, making him appear younger than he was, a decision that began his spiral into an abyss. Late in life my father told me, as he reevaluated his relationship with his parents, that they bought poorly-done papers, easily recognizable as forgeries. Maybe haste clouded their judgment, maybe it was all they could afford, maybe it was an eruption of Dutch thrift in a difficult time. In any case, his identity redone by the graphic skills of an over-confident seventeen-year-old boy from the neighbourhood, he left.

Inevitably, on January 3, 1945, he was arrested by the *Sicherheitspolizei*, near the town of Elburg – about 150 kilometres from Loosduinen, with only another sixty kilometres to go. His arrest won't feature as one of the War's heroic narratives. He wasn't caught in an act of brave resistance, of hiding Jews, say, or working for the Underground. It was an ordinary arrest at the time, an ordinary catastrophe. But in its ordinariness it is moving and important on its own terms, and it is maybe a more timeless story, a story of a person just trying to stay alive, and a bungled attempt to do so.

After his arrest, my father was imprisoned in solitary confinement in a five-by-ten-foot cell and interrogated for about a week. Rather than reveal the name of the person who falsified his papers, he claimed he had done the work himself. He was then transported to and imprisoned in *Polizeiliches Durchgangslager Amersfoort* – Kamp Amersfoort. On his arrival on January 13 he was made to give up his clothing, sign over his money and affirm that he had no other valuables. Then he was entered into the camp records, issued a mess kit, wooden shoes, and prison clothes, including a thin overcoat – the clothes hand-me-downs from previous generations of prisoners who had since been transported to Germany, either for forced labour or extermination. On the front of his coat was a red triangle, indicating he was a political prisoner; on the back a large red dot, a different kind of sign, indicating that he was a dangerous risk for escaping, and making it easier for him to be shot if he ever tried. He was assigned to Barrack 4 and sent to the barber to have his head shaved. He was now prisoner 10090.

Located in the centre of the Netherlands near a major rail hub, *Polizeiliches Durchgangslager Amersfoort* looked much like other Nazi concentration or prison camps. It had the necessary infrastructure for daily life: administrative offices, storage areas, a kitchen, sick ward, barber shop, and outdoor latrines. Since it was outfitted for the daily life of a prison camp, there were also eight watchtowers with searchlights, guards, and machine guns placed around the perimeter of a ten-foot-high barbed wire fence. Outside of the fence were the rifle range and the mortuary. As well as separate cells for solitary confinement, Amersfoort had five barracks for the prisoners, with crude bunks stacked three high and small stoves for heat. Barrack 4, my father's barrack, was divided into four sections, each holding about 150 prisoners. Each bunk was equipped with a thin straw mattress and a horse blanket. My father was assigned the top bed of the fourth bunk to the left of the entrance. A large bell would summon prisoners to the centre of camp life, an area of scenes of ritual terror – a parade square for *appel* (roll call, three times a day). Amersfoort also had one feature unique to it: a narrow passage of barbed wire with more barbed wire laid loosely on the ground, which the guards called the *rozentuin* (rose garden). Prisoners were brought there to stand rigid, without food or water, for up to twenty-four hours, in sight of the other prisoners. If they fell they were beaten.

Amersfoort was both a detention and a transit camp; prisoners were incarcerated there as punishment, but also to be sent on later to Germany to work or, on one occasion, to be executed. Over the course of the War more than 47,000 people were imprisoned in Amersfoort. Most stayed for a period of just a few days or weeks before being sent to their fate in Germany. Amersfoort was not one of the big extermination factories of the War. Yet even though it was designed as a transit and punishment camp, the National Monument Camp Amersfoort has established that there were more executions and deaths here than at any other place in the Netherlands – at least 662 prisoners died over the course of the War, at times with formal executions, but often unpredictably, with a sudden raid on a barrack, and someone dragged out in the middle of the night; or with someone being dragged out on the appel ground to be beaten to death in front of the other prisoners, death not through the intervention of a scheduled bullet at a distance, but death more personal and vindictive, the angry satisfactions of repeated blows of the butt of a rifle or the kicks of a polished boot. Amersfoort was a place of rage, a place where horror and death could erupt for no apparent reason, at any time. And, of course, it being both a punishment and a transit camp, many more perished after being transported from Amersfoort to Germany for forced labour or extermination.

My father arrived at a bad time. Having been briefly closed, Amersfoort was reopened in May 1943 on a larger scale, with a dramatic increase in the numbers imprisoned for attempting to escape Nazi conscription. The barracks were overcrowded and often chaotic. The administration had also changed, more vindictive and at times out of control, with drunken and psychotic rages on the part of some – about the time my father was imprisoned, it is reported that one prisoner was buried alive. When the War was all but lost, in March of 1945, Karl Peter Berg, Amersfoort's commandant, had forty-nine men executed in revenge for an assault on Hanns Albin Rauter (the *SS und Polizeiführer* in the Netherlands) and threw their bodies into a mass grave.

More involved in daily matters was Joseph Kotälla, the "Executioner of Amersfoort," an SS officer whose deadly kicks to the groin were so famous they were named after him (the "Kotälla Kick"). He was seriously unstable; even after his appointment to Amersfoort he was temporarily admitted by the Nazis to a hospital for psychiatric treatment, and then returned to work. On New Year's Day 1945, two days before my father was arrested near Elburg, Kotälla, in a rage over the escape of two prisoners, forced a large group of prisoners to lie on the icy ground during appel, where they were whipped and beaten. According to prisoner witnesses, Kotälla danced and jumped on the bodies of the prisoners, kicking them in the head, breaking their ankles, and stomping on their spines. He did it silently, without laughing or yelling. Around one hundred prisoners were left so badly injured that they were taken to the hospital barracks that day.

After my father was admitted, his routine set in. Amersfoort's prisoners were given hard, physical work, in the cold and imposed on starving bodies, work designed to squeeze out the last bit of utility from another human being. My father was assigned to the outdoor work detail, in a cold winter, with inadequate clothing. His thin overcoat had no shirt or sweater underneath it, and the clothing, which may have been in decent shape at the beginning of the War, was in tatters by 1945, having been used and reused by each new batch of arrivals.[3] Among his work party were Jewish prisoners, awaiting their transport to extermination camps further east. The outdoor work detail was not a privilege. The overseer was brutal, and beatings and harassment dominated the day.[4] My father's attachment to this detail was by his own request, but a decision of naïveté rather than solidarity. Upon arriving at Amersfoort as a sixteen-year-old boy he volunteered for the outside detail, having always enjoyed physical outdoor work. The work was so cruel and physically devastating that other prisoners would at times share their own meagre food with those unfortunate enough to be in this detail. After being marched to the work site, my father's detail would begin their day by building a fire to keep the guards warm, and then set to the main work. My father's job, along with the hundred other prisoners in his detail, was to fell trees, trim them, saw them into usable lengths, and carry some of it back on his shoulder to camp each day. The mode of carrying was highly regulated and overseen by the guards. My father recalls the heavy carrying to be painful, pressing down on his bones. One day he shifted his load to alleviate the pain, was caught in the act, and was beaten with a stick.

Before prisoners went out to work, each day there was morning appel. Appel, three times a day, was mandatory, and the evening appel could take hours, to check for possible escapees. Dinner would be late on those days. At the sound of Amersfoort's camp bell all prisoners, under the threat of a beating, assembled on the appel ground. Prisoners were made to stand outside, still and silent for hours in the cold, sometimes naked, while the guards counted and recounted them. My father noted that the guards often were most numerically challenged on the coldest days and had to take breaks from their counting to warm up inside.

Former prisoners recall the appels as being the worst moments of the day. Prisoners were severely reprimanded for the slightest infractions, and the punishments were horrific. Those to be punished were hauled in front of the other prisoners, who were then forced to watch the beatings and hear the screams. They had to watch the beatings unmoving, rigid, not turning their eyes away. My father remembers watching someone being beaten to death, someone who had missed appel and whom Kotälla kicked in the groin so hard that it killed him.

My father recalled one morning as he was leaving the barracks for appel he and a fellow prisoner noticed another man still lying down, too weak to stand. Knowing that people who did not attend appel would be severely beaten, perhaps to death, they carried him to the appel grounds, found a place in the middle of the group, and propped him up between them. Prisoners during appel were not allowed to touch each other, and if discovered, they would be punished. But they held him up, trying to hide surrounded by the other prisoners, while the guards went slowly round three times, counting and recounting.

Killings were part of camp routine. Some seemed random: my father reports that the guards would occasionally enter the barracks at night, pull two or three prisoners out into the darkness, and shoot them. The prisoner in the bunk next to my father suffered this fate. Other public killings were more formal, with condemned prisoners marched down to the specially prepared execution grounds. The path to the grounds, and the grounds themselves, had been dug in the sandy hilly area just outside the camp to a length of 350 metres, primarily by Jewish prisoners. As with the rose garden and the beatings at appel, these executions were meant to terrorize. One of my father's more traumatic memories was of being assembled on the appel ground to witness three prisoners being marched to be shot, and their defiantly singing a verse from Psalm 43 (a psalm pleading for God to rescue the psalmist from the "deceitful and wicked," to vindicate him "against an unfaithful nation") on their way to the deaths they knew were coming:

> *Dan ga ik op tot Gods altaren,*
> *Tot God, mijn God, de bron van vreugd;*
> *Dan zal ik, juichend, stem en snaren*
> *Ten roem van zijne goedheid paren,*
> *Die, na kortstondig' ongeneugt,*
> *Mij eindeloos verheugt.*
>
> (Then I will go to the altars of God,
> To God, my God, the source of joy;
> Then I will jubilantly pair my voice with my strings
> To the glory of His goodness,
> Who, after momentary displeasure,
> endlessly delights me.)

At such moments, my father said, many decades later, he and others had a kind of feeling of jealousy: "Those about to be killed were at the end of the road, and we still had to carry on." He was at the point, he said, where "I wanted to get it over with."

Het Boek der Psalmen, *Gereformeerde Kerk van Nederland, 1938 printing of 1773 authorization*

In the face of this despair my father had his spiritual routines, which he later testified kept him alive. He and three other Christians from different denominations, including a Roman Catholic priest, shared memorized hymns and Bible passages, in temporary islands of grace which were precious to him, and which, once he began speaking of Amersfoort, he mentioned often. Every night he and the three prayed for strength if their time should come to be taken out and executed. This spiritual practice did not keep everyone in the group alive: one of the four was shot while trying to escape, and one other died of dysentery and exhaustion after being transported to Germany.

It was not just the extreme cold, inadequate clothing, harsh work, punishments, and dehumanization that ground at the core of prisoners' humanity. There was almost no food. During much of the War the official rations that were to sustain prisoners through their days consisted of a weak coffee in the morning, at noon a bowl of potato soup, and in the evening a small piece of bread. Near the end of my father's incarceration, things got even more meagre, and he was limited to one small bun and one bowl of watery potato soup per day. One day a food shipment arrived from the Red Cross, with two sandwiches for each prisoner. Commandant Berg ordered that the prisoners each take their own sandwiches, march to the camp pigsty, throw the sandwiches to the pigs, and watch the pigs eat them. My father lost more than thirty pounds in the five weeks he was in custody.

On the evening of January 31 my father was scheduled to be sent to Germany – he and his fellow prisoners believed they were being sent to Neuengamme, near Hamburg, a concentration camp well within German borders, out of reach of the Allies. As a condition of his transport, he was compelled to sign a form declaring that he would never speak of what he had experienced in Kamp Amersfoort, under pain of harsh punishment. The evening of his transport was cold, just one or two degrees above freezing and raining off and on. It was to be his last formal appel. There he was, forced to stand outside for more than an hour, in freezing weather, naked, one of the youngest of the 226 prisoners waiting to be given back their civilian clothes so that they could be transported to Germany. They were then marched through the silent town of Amersfoort to the train station. The marching from Kamp Amersfoort happened at night now, in the dark, partly to avoid Allied war planes, but also because on one occasion earlier in the War when prisoners were brought to the station in the daytime (before the town's night curfew restricted people to their homes), the women of the town defiantly came out with sandwiches and a cap or other clothing for the men (the cap to hide the shaved head and make escape easier), many of whom were being sent to die.[5] So, my father and his fellow prisoners marched to the station in the dark, and there they waited and waited, but no train came. As a result, they were marched back to Kamp Amersfoort, where an administrative stalemate ensued, since they had already been formally released. They were not on the rolls anymore. From having been reduced to prisoner 10090, he now no longer officially existed. He and the others were hustled back into the camp and confined to barracks until the next transport train, but since they were not technically prisoners, my father told me they received no food during the week they waited. The ledgers wouldn't be able to account for it. When the train to Germany finally arrived on February 5 – a day on which twenty prisoners were shot – it moved very slowly, which many prisoners used as an opportunity to attempt to escape. They were unaware, however, that guards were stationed on the last train car. Anyone who dared to escape was shot at, and many of them died. The National Archive in the Hague reveals that of the 226 prisoners who left Kamp Amersfoort on the fifth, only 165 arrived in Germany. One of the dead was a man known to me only as Jan, one of my father's group of four, who leapt from the train while it was crossing a river, hoping the water would save him, only to be machine-gunned to death. My father wanted to join in the escape, but he was too frail, and his fingers, having been frozen from his outdoor work during his time in Kamp Amersfoort, were too fragile to allow him to steady himself for the jump. So he stayed, and saved his life.

The trip ended at the recently bombed German town of Gronau, just across the Dutch border. The scene was chaotic, with people screaming and running frantically when he arrived. The locomotive, having also suffered damage, could go no further, so there they sat. Eventually, the guards marched them to a local school to wait while things got sorted out. And then dysentery further ravaged the bodies of some prisoners, becoming an occasion for further cruelty. Late in his life, my father would tell and retell this most traumatic experience of his incarceration. If a prisoner did not make it to the latrine in time, guards would compel him to eat his own excrement. My father, having contracted dysentery, avoided this grotesque humiliation, but he was forced to watch someone else being compelled to do so, under the supervision of two smiling SS men. As his fellow prisoner slowly ate he stared directly at my father and held his gaze. Along with the voices of those being marched to execution, those silent despairing eyes, sunken into a shaved head, stayed with my father and tormented him more than anything else.

After the Red Cross inspected the school where my father was imprisoned, they warned the Nazis that, unless the dysentery was treated or isolated, it would spread into the town. With one prisoner already having died of it, my father and three others were then released to the Red Cross to receive medical care (according to records at the Dutch National Archive, another prisoner was left behind to die). They were brought back just across the German border, back to the Netherlands, to a makeshift hospital in the town of Enschede. There, my father's frozen fingers were operated on, without anesthetic, the doctors slicing into his hand to cut out the gangrene that had begun to form. With my father still under German guard, a nurse somehow managed to get him his release papers. They were his second set of false documents for the winter of 1945: as a strategy to keep him from being arrested again, the staff gave him an official document stating that he was released because he suffered from tuberculosis and epilepsy. And he was free to go.

With the train lines out in Enschede, some members of the staff assisted my father on a ten-kilometre walk to the town of Hengelo, where he hoped to board a train in the direction of Koekange. As he stood there at the station, someone called out his name: a friend of his brother Theo, and the friend's father, on their way to rural Friesland in the north, where there still was food. The friend was a welcome sight, but the father, a known Nazi sympathizer, was a bit iffy. And yet. They helped him, the father giving him a cap to hide his shaved head and boarding the train with him, since they were going in the same direction. On the train, an altercation: two women had carried their bicycles aboard, which was against regulations. German soldiers attempted to confiscate the bicycles, an act which degenerated into shouting and chaos, with the result that they arrested everyone in the car, ordering them to get off at the next stop. At that stop, the soldiers rounded up and began to question everyone, but in the commotion my father and his companions began to run. There were shots fired, but they ran – over a fence, down a side street, across a bridge – and made it safely away, with twelve more kilometres for my father to walk, alone, with what he thought was the smell of death on him. And then, nearing his grandfather's house in Koekange, he saw his mother and younger brother Theo outside, shaking the dust out of a carpet. An ordinary domestic scene. It was February 14, 1945. He was home. He probably thought his War was over.

*

From a distance, he called out "Moeder! Moeder!" His mother paused her work, having heard somebody shout something she couldn't make out. Looking up, she saw an ill-clothed, dirty, emaciated man. Assuming he was a beggar, she took Theo by the hand, went into the house, and closed the door.

Me and the house in Koekange, 2007

TELLING HIS STORY

The Gory Details

AFTER ALL THIS, after the door in Koekange closes a second time and this time he is safe inside, once the eruption of Amersfoort seems to recede and its ash starts to settle, how does one come to terms with the eruption itself? As my father's life stretched before him and Amersfoort moved from pure sensation and into a remembered past, he felt the need for it to *mean* something. He needed a way to think about starving and throwing his food to pigs, standing naked in the rain, watching a man being kicked to death. What, in one's trauma, becomes emblematic, and what do these things mean? How does horror become a *story*? These are also questions for me, living with him and now writing this memoir. My relation to his story, how to understand and then how to tell it, has always been fraught, in ways that are at times transparently obvious, at other times baffling. It's not as simple as his story becoming my story, that I took on a replicated form of his trauma; it's more that *struggling with his story* became my story, difficult in its own peculiar way. Only in the past few years, after hearing my father describe his own ambivalent attitude to telling his story, have I begun to understand the pressures on memory and on telling as one struggles to make trauma mean something.

How to deal with what had happened in Kamp Amersfoort would trouble my father for the rest of his life;

increasingly there were fraught moments, later in his life and after decades of silence, when he found himself more and more compulsively telling disconnected moments of his story, as an attempt to shake off or explain Amersfoort's hold on his mind and body. In his ending years, exhausted by his suffering and its demands, he would occasionally voice his frustration – not so much about what had happened to him, but about his sometime-listeners. With impatient scorn, he would say that when people in his retirement home asked to hear his story, "They just want to hear the gory details." Hearing this, I was startled both by the contempt in the voice of the gentlest man I knew, and because up until this moment he had never characterized his experience in these terms.

What made him snap, if only briefly? Probably it was a mixture of the stresses near the end of his life: his health, including the standard problems of a failing heart, deafness, and increasingly weak balance and eyesight, but also his uncontrollable shaking and anxiety; the fatigue of dealing with the press of his memories, which increasingly encroached on both his sleep and his waking moments; and his deteriorating relationship with my mother, a situation which began to rival Amersfoort in his mind, as well as trigger his shaking and flashbacks. But there was also something else gnawing at him, something that had gradually come into focus about his War experience: people's attitudes to his stories were not what he had hoped for, and it wore him down. Bad enough to spend time in a concentration camp without also having people be obtuse about how to respond to his living with and speaking of it. His recent disconnect with his audience seemed to arise from the distance – seventy-five years and more – between his time in Amersfoort and his final years in the rest home. Perhaps with the danger of the War receding from people's psyches it had increasingly became just history, and he and his experience a rarity. In any event, he sensed their interest was tinged with voyeurism about the shocking details. He thought his curious listeners wanted only part of his story, paring it down, simplifying it according to their desires: they "just wanted to hear" the riveting parts. This new response disturbed him. They didn't get the genre right. For his whole life he had wanted his story to be something other than a thing of prurient curiosity. That desire is what drove him on the only two occasions he told his story in an extended form (once as a testimony in a church, and the other about five years after that when he wrote a short book about his life). Of course, he knew the details of his incarceration were shocking, but he wanted his story and his life to have a shape, to have dignity; he wanted its gory details to serve a larger story, to be placed in the context of his belief that God's protection had sustained and saved him during that awful period. From the moment he reached safety in Koekange he understood – or needed – Amersfoort to be a redemption story, to have a narrative arc, so that others would understand the greatness of God. He didn't aim for it to be someone's "trauma porn."

Maybe my father was attempting an impossible task. Gory details are inescapable in trauma narratives, and their hold is tight, almost painful, at times hard to move beyond, knocking the rest of the story off balance. In movies, novels, memoirs, the horror of the details often blocks one's path with shock, shock that this unimaginable thing really happened, in this way, to another human being; and in the moment it throws everything off-kilter and horror inevitably takes over, seizing you and short-circuiting for a time, anyway, empathy and the possibility of a closed narrative. It is all so far beyond your experience, so unimaginable. This was brought home to me while reading Daniel Mendelsohn's *The Lost: A Search for Six of Six Million*, an account of Mendelsohn's relentless search to find out what happened to six members of his uncle's family, how they died, murdered in German-occupied Poland during the Holocaust. His book rhythmically oscillates between desultory movement and violent jolts of horror, moments which are both gripping and unbearable. Over the course of Mendelsohn's narrative the moment arrives when he needs to write about the murder of his cousin Ruchele. His description is shocking and gruesome, and he presses it home by describing the final movement to her death in a single sentence that came at me like a tsunami, phrase on phrase, relentlessly stretching for hundreds of words, holding me in its grip, never letting me go, until finally it crashed to an end, with Ruchele at the end of a plank above a mass grave, naked, waiting to be shot.[6] Horrified, I couldn't stop reading, gulping down the prose, and at this moment my reading wasn't about learning facts; it wasn't about ethics, or even empathy. It was just a surge within me, a visceral shock. I have never been more relieved to have a sentence come to an end.

That eruption of shock in my reading of *The Lost*, coupled with my father's occasional anger at his audience, has helped me understand my own instabilities in how I responded to and occasionally told the story of my father's War – a trauma story at a remove, one might think, a story told not by the man who suffered, with the events physically stamped on his body, but by his child, who lived in the shadow of his trauma. But entangled as I have been in listening to or uncovering the details of his story (with the ethical turbulence I have described via Mendelsohn's writing and my father's scornful reaction to his listeners), the occasions of my *re*telling his story of trauma have always been fraught. They pull in opposing directions, both intensely primal but also theatrical in their weird rituals and overwrought emotion.

Sometimes my father's story is squeezed out of me by others, and at other times the telling happens when something inside compels me to spill as much as I can stand – and it is spilling; there is nothing pretty or measured about it. Both tellings have an internal push and simultaneous resistance that feels like the attraction/repulsion of porn. It is all unbalanced and unsettled, a visceral mess that grips not just my mind, but my body.

Sometimes, over the course of my adult life, people have just asked. Knowing something about my parents, that they were old and frail and had health issues, they would ask the normal, broad question: how they were doing. Instead of just saying "fine," a response which would be evasive at best, I, propelled by some unknown inner urging, would occasionally tell the truth, that my father was not doing well. I knew what I had just done, and kind of hoped it would stop there, but of course my response prompted sympathy and further questions of varying specificity, and in response at times I would state, or feel compelled to blurt, that his health was failing because his PTSD had become more than his body and mind could bear. And then there was no stepping back, and all the steps went downhill, faster and faster.

For example, in the year before my father's death, one day I spent part of an afternoon hanging around with a few others in a church kitchen after a funeral, after cleaning up the remnants of the reception. The dishes loaded into the industrial washer, the tea towels hung to dry, and the floor given a cursory mopping, we began to chat as we waited for the last few coffee cups. After those preliminary questions and answers about my father's health, things began to speed up, three different people asking one question after another, about my father's age at the time, about the location of the camp, about the reason for his arrest, about how it all ended, digging further and further into my father's trauma. To anyone watching I'm sure the questions looked calm, curious but not invasive, but to me they felt rapid-fire, and I wanted to duck, realizing I didn't want to be here, trapped here in the place I had put myself. But, as it always happened, given my panicky state, once the process had started there was no way to cut off questions without being weird, and no way to bust out of the kitchen without bodily moving people out of my way. Being odd in that way didn't feel like an option. Instead, I looked down, as I always did, avoiding eye contact while I gave my answers about what happened to my father years ago, my answers clipped, short as I could make them, given in a flat voice, with me trying to will it to all stop. But no one seemed to pick up on it, oblivious to the weight and danger of their questions. Eventually they did stop, having moved on to other topics, and I got out of there. I walked home drained and exhausted, terribly sad. I didn't want to talk to Susan, my wife, about what had happened. Instead, I remained inside myself and headed for bed early, quietly. (Even while writing the first draft of this, from a distance of several weeks, I felt the tension rising, my breath becoming more rapid and shallow again, my pulse more noticeable.) Fight or flight is a terrible set of alternatives, even in a church kitchen.

Other times over the years I would instigate the telling, under the pressure of who knows what. It was not the nudge of a casual instinct to keep a conversation going that prompted me, but an almost physical pressure. The need to tell would surge up, trying to relieve the pressure of a secondhand albatross hanging around my neck. Again, I would start to panic as I recounted my father's horrible suffering during the War. Everything was muddled, and pushed in an odd direction. Sure, I loved him, I really, deeply loved him, and his suffering had been more than anyone could deal with. But his suffering was not just a testament to him and an occasion for my sympathy and others' empathy; it was also somehow an occasion of my own danger, and on these occasions too I performed my own homely enactments of the classic fight or flight reactions. Again, I would look down, shoulders up, heart rate high, my breathing shallow. I would tell my father's suffering oddly, feeling aggressive, angry and defiant towards either the story or these kind people, who were probably baffled at the manner of my telling. My purpose was unfocussed. At times I would want to trot out all the gory details, at other times not. (And I never told it as a story of God's care; under the pressure of the moment I couldn't find myself reaching for it or any other standard interpretive frame.) But whatever happened, what I was doing was urgent, panicked. To call it unburdening is too neat; my telling was not only weirdly physical and emotionally messy, it was polemical. It was not just that I wanted to spread the news, hold people by their shoulders, shake them, and shout, "This is *important*!" It was also that being forced to hear my father's – *my* – story, my listeners validated him, and they validated me. An odd strategy – talking about Amersfoort, about events that happened fifteen years before I was born, as my way of saying I am important. And why would I need to do that, and give myself weight via someone else's experience in a Nazi prison camp as my evidence? How was this not just a tawdry form of appropriation, with all the imbalance and lack of proportion that implies?

My purposes were always muddled, and if I am honest, I think that most of the time I told my father's story I didn't even want my listener's sympathy. I wanted something else, and my goals didn't line up with those of my listeners. Genre confusion messed everything up: my listeners thought they were hearing about my father and about history, while I, under great and messy duress, was telling them not just about my father's trauma, but also my trauma, a trauma which gave me dignity because it separated me from the ordinary lives of my listeners and gave some redemption to or justification of the difficult childhood years of living with and under the shadow of my father and his War. Unsurprisingly, these were not occasions for reciprocity. I didn't want my listeners to offer an account of an uncle who had to hide in a cellar, or grandparents who hid Jews. I felt churlish. To my mind that was history for them, a riveting story, an anecdote to be shared. Their stories were not analogous to the story of my father, and to my telling of it. Their heart rate didn't increase while they spoke; their shoulders didn't tighten and rise, pressing into a stiffening neck; their breathing remained calm and even. The rest of their day would be fine. And why wouldn't it? They didn't live with their story; it was not traumatic to them; it was not written into their bodies. Those differences were and remain stark to me, and so, I didn't want my listeners near the place I was *in*, looking at this from the same level as me. They hadn't done the work, they hadn't lived it.

And after having once again told my father's story, with intense and contrasting emotions and a body shimmering with anxiety, I would feel flat, and want to leave, be left alone, and go lie down. Everybody could just fuck off. What did they know?

Memory

DURING THESE MESSY encounters I would tell only part of my father's story, at most barely gesturing to what his experience of living with the War for all his following decades was like, and remaining tight-lipped about my own memories of those years. These are memories I do not tell to listeners in a church kitchen. The memories come at me from surprising corners, at times: while she was digitizing some of my parents' photographs recently, my sister Elisabeth texted me a photo. It was a photo from my childhood in Edmonton, the city to where my parents had moved after the War. In the top right corner, there I sit, in a pew near the front of a packed church with the rest of my family. I am eleven years old, a skinny kid, pure white hair cut shorter than I wanted, wearing a new off-white coat that was nice, but too crisp and not quite in style. A little too fussy. And those glasses, more often than not broken and held together with scotch tape. (They were my last pair with regular plastic frames. The next glasses were to be stronger and somehow in style, but they ended up an amalgam of my frustrated attempts to be cool and my immigrant mother, like all immigrant mothers, always getting it slightly wrong. I wanted wires, those thin round John Lennon wires. Instead, I was given glasses with metal alright, but glasses with aluminum temples, thick, shiny, and unbreakable.) My father isn't in the pew with us. He is right at the front of the church, near the right edge of the picture, standing straight, holding up a flag on a staff. It is Monday, May 4, 1970, the day before the twenty-fifth *Bevrijdingsdag*, the day the Netherlands was finally freed of Nazi control. For this one year, anyway, the Dutch community in Edmonton got together for a memorial to celebrate. That reference didn't register on me. But I knew it was an occasion. We had driven out in the evening, on a school night, to a fancy downtown church – not the community-built one we worshipped in on Sundays, but something bigger, grander, strange and solemn, something needing pillars – probably Anglican. There was a procession, and my father came in, carrying a flag and stopping up front, motionless, waiting for something to happen. I don't remember anything more about the ceremony other than that, but I knew it was serious. The digitized picture reveals more to me than my scattered memory can.

But I do remember the trip home. After whatever occasion we were marking ended, our family piled into the car and headed for home. I sat in the back middle seat, as the youngest and smallest, my legs not pushed up by the hump of the driveshaft. As we drove home in silence, I began a short conversation, asking my mother, "Why did Dad carry the flag, why was he with some others up front?"

Her reply: "That was for people who hid during the War."

"Where did you hide, Dad?"

My father immediately broke down, convulsively crying, head bowed. And then, from beside me, came just one sharp word, percussive and hissed, from one of my sisters:

"Len!"

Nothing more was needed or said, just this short accusatory reprimand. It was clear that I had opened something up that should stay closed, that I had done and precipitated

Edmonton, Alberta
May 4, 1970, *the day before* Bevrijdingsdag

something shameful. Did my sister, a few years older than I, know what was going on when she scolded me, did she know we must never refer to the War, or was she just aware that I had made my father cry, that crying was shameful, and that it was my fault? All I knew was that I had poked at something dangerous. My father collected himself and kept driving, looking straight ahead. We went on in silence again, in the dark, and when we arrived home nobody spoke of what had happened. No one clarified anything; whatever guilt or confusion I felt was something I would have to deal with alone. We all just went to bed. It was late for a school night.

*

Another memory, another time: decades later, I in my fifties now, on a winter day in a warm and quiet sunlit room talking with a therapist, sorting out how to deal with my recurrent eruptions of depression and anxiety. As always, the talk turned to my relationship with my father, and his experiences in the War. It was a tough session, but I was assured that my increasing agitation that day was somehow the sign of excellent progress. And suddenly, a gulf opened up. As it had happened regularly in my life when the War erupted, my breathing became careful and deliberate, and I sat very still, neck stiff, looking straight ahead though nothing in the room was in my focus. I was looking elsewhere. I had remembered something, and I was seeing it clearly. It was our kitchen, and I was maybe seven years old. My father standing still, his head bowed, weeping and paralyzed. My mother whirling in desperation, desperation which at times seemed like anger, shouting at my brother to take my father to Oliver, a local psychiatric hospital. She didn't know what to do anymore.

My brother, maybe sixteen or so, just standing there, silent and immobile. I can see him, wearing a red plaid shirt and blue jeans, with his skinny leather belt that was too long for his narrow waist. Even with my mother's whirling, everyone was paralyzed, locked in panicky stasis. And I was just watching, frozen, next to the kitchen counter, unnoticed in the background. As I sat in the sunlit room recalling the scene, an event I had never remembered before that day, everything stopped, a bottom fell out, and I was hovering over a deep black hole. The office became deathly silent. I ended the session abruptly – I mumbled something, paid my fee, and walked home.

But that memory – the kitchen, the whirling desperation, the weeping paralysis – is a memory of something that never happened. After thinking about that scene over the years and its connections to other memories, and after speaking to my brother recently (not that we speak very often of my father's War), it has become clear its vividness isn't that of a real memory. It was something different, its meaning hidden in what the experience felt like. Its stasis and staginess had the qualities of a tableau, signifying recurring things in our family: my mother's angry desperation, my father's weeping paralysis, and my brother's immobility, being commanded to do something that a child should never be asked to do. And me – there in that kitchen, and as I would be so many times in my life, even sixty years later in a different quiet sunlit room, with my father in his rest home – me on the sidelines, thousands of miles from home, watching, trying to figure things out, how they fit together, what they meant, and mean.

My childhood memories of how I experienced or came to know my father's trauma as a child and young adult are all like the two I have just described: broken images, narratively sketchy, unresolved, silent in their unconnected sudden appearance and disappearance – little narrative and no trajectory, just sensation and, because of their brevity and disconnection, an anxious epistemological quandary. The memories that I narrate here, of my childhood and early adulthood spent trying to understand what happened to my father and how it shaped him and me have a characteristic form and affect. Each one is like a tableau, like one of those staged and motionless dramatic recreations of famous moments in history or art, each figure locked into place at an intense moment extracted from a larger context. True to the genre, my scattered tableau memories are immediate and sensuous, but silent and severed from the context around them, their meanings constricted by their structure and cordoned off by their boundaries, without the trajectories and complications of narrative. Noiseless, they are observed from a distance, and not from within, as a participant. But for all that, not inexpressive. These severed memories are powerful precisely because of their disconnection. Their stasis and distance create an emotional charge, and a search for what is arrested, what is timeless, what it signifies, and what has been left out on either side. In their minimalism they offer their own kind of meaning, meaning based on resistance against completeness, redemption. And they certainly encapsulate my *experience* of things.

KAMP AMERSFOORT: AFTERWARDS

Silence

A FEW YEARS before he died, my father silently got up from his chair, walked across the living room to open a drawer, and after a short search showed me a letter from 1945, a letter he had saved but had shown nobody for maybe sixty years. It is the one letter he was permitted to write home to his family while imprisoned. It is in his neat handwriting, the return address given as Polizeiliches Durchgangslager Amersfoort, Block 10, No. 10090. It is curious to look at – written in faint pencil but traced over with pen, tracing which has physically pressed into the thin yellowed paper in places. Soon after the War, my father said, he did the tracing himself, worried that the pencil would fade over time, and the letter's contents lost. This odd palimpsest did not erase history, but inscribed it more forcefully, an overwriting of the original time by a determined response to that time. This, at least, would be one record that would not disappear. It is an astoundingly evasive letter that completely fills the allowed space, a space surveilled, of course, by his Nazi captors. As were all prisoners, my father was warned to reveal nothing negative. Thus, the task for prisoners was to write a letter that allowed its recipients, in my father's words, to "read the real message between the lines." The undated letter begins blandly, with my father asking his family how they are doing and hoping that they are still well. He then reports that with him "everything is in order," and that he has plenty to eat. After asking his mother if she still suffers from anxiety, he writes that he is in God's hands, who will make everything clear in the end, as they all know. In any event, he hopes to be speedily released. He asks about each of his siblings in turn – if his younger brother is back in school, if his sister is helping around the house, and if they will give his baby brother a kiss from him. He asks to extend his greetings to all his acquaintances, and his mother to write quickly in return. In his closing he tells his mother not to worry, and to pray for strength – for whose strength is unclear. The letter has silences which hover over it, silences more expressive than the penciled words on the thin paper.

Without the silences it is a very ordinary letter. Other than the request for prayers and strength, it could be a letter home from summer camp. One thing is missing: according to Amersfoort policy he was allowed to ask for twenty guilders per month to buy extra food. My father doesn't mention money – this despite his weakness and near starvation. It may be due to nervousness about what his captors might think, or an attempt to keep his parents from worry, or that there was no money to be sent, or if sent it wouldn't arrive, or that it might not arrive before he was transported further down the line into Germany, or if it did arrive on time he would not be allowed to use it – but whatever that silence means is now unknowable. In any case, the silence had no practical consequences back then. Perhaps due to the disorganization of the postal service near the end of the War, or an error in the mailroom at Amersfoort, or a plausible Amersfoort policy to hold back mail until prisoners were released or dead or transported out of reach to Germany, my father's letters did not arrive until he had been home for about a month. The letter is postmarked March 17, which, as my father pointed out to me, is also his birthday.

Letter home, Winter 1945

Shortly after he wrote that letter my father was free, ready to restart his life, looking ahead, not back. The War was over, and Amersfoort would not figure in this new life. Everyone wanted it to disappear. So silence descended over the events at Amersfoort; or rather, a silence was clamped over it, with only my father living and dealing with what had happened, Amersfoort caged within him. Speaking of that initial silence years later, he told me that it was "a very lonely time for me when I came back to Loosduinen. Nobody wanted to talk about it." It wasn't a comfortable silence for him. After his welcome home his parents never spoke to him of it again. On his return to Loosduinen the pastor of his church promised a visit that, though scheduled and then rescheduled twice, never happened.

My father also saved from that time one other letter, this one from his father, written about a month after his return from Amersfoort. (His father, a psychiatric nurse, was not with the family, having been evacuated from the West with his patients to the relative safety of Arnhem, where he was put in more danger in the wake of the disastrous Allied campaign of Operation Market Garden.) The occasion of his father's letter is to wish him a happy seventeenth birthday. Nestled in that letter, which I first saw when my father was in his nineties, is a short reference to Amersfoort – to the time of the incarceration, which his father believes my father will not easily forget, but of which my grandfather, of course, knows nothing, and whose ravages he can only imagine. He exhorts my father to join him in thanking God that this difficult time didn't last any longer. He wishes to talk to my father about his imprisonment, and also to tell him of his own experience during that time, of unsuccessfully searching for him, and promises they will find an occasion to talk about all that. And then he pivots to other issues. It being March and things winding down, he hopes the War will end soon, and then offers my father some help in finding work. Time to turn to new things. The letter ends with renewed wishes for a happy birthday.

Other than the letter my father wrote from Amersfoort, this is the only document he saved from that time. Why? It was not for the birthday wishes, or the offers of help in employment, or a general affectionate remembrance of his father. When he first showed me the letter, he pointed out that the promised talk, like all the other promised talks from that time, never materialized. In his mid-eighties he would begin to speak with bitterness about his family's silence, a silence to which his father's letter testifies. His family's imposed silence was tenacious, extending even to physical reminders. As soon as my father returned home, his father insisted on immediately returning the sling for his damaged hand to the Enschede hospital, and also returned his forged ID card, it rightly being property of the government, he said. (My mother had a different take. At ninety-nine years old, in her first reference to me about the forged card, she said that my father's parents should never have trusted the famous overconfidence of the forger's family, and that his parents wanted to get rid of the card's embarrassing presence.)

That silence never left his family. Decades later, a few years after he began serious treatment for his trauma, my father began writing about that period, and sent the resulting short book to his mother and siblings in the Netherlands. He told me that they never gave any evidence of having read it.

*

While the silence initially was imposed on my father (despite his early feelings of loneliness), he didn't remain its unwilling participant. After a time, and for many years, he believed in and enacted it. To heal, one needed to forget. But while one could avoid speaking of Amersfoort, the Netherlands was filled with physical reminders of the War. So, eight years after the War he and his wife and two small children emigrated, in the face of his own mother's vociferous opposition. With two stops for refueling, they flew across the ocean, landed in Montreal, and boarded a train for a trip of three days and nights, west across the wild and disorienting northern edge of Lake Superior, and then across the endless prairies, and north up to Edmonton, Alberta. Their trip was more than three times the distance from Loosduinen to Moscow, and with an added ocean between. No other family members emigrated with them. From Edmonton, the War must have seemed like it had happened in another world. So, my father took the silence with him, to Canada.

This new world, for all its difficulties, must have felt something like hope. But its difficulties were real. In their first few years my parents moved from place to place, the most difficult of their temporary homes being a renovated chicken coop in the Bush Mine farm, a site in the North Saskatchewan River Valley of a former coal mine and farm whose buildings had been repurposed. The place was so cold that ice formed on the inside of the windows, and my mother at times warmed her baby daughter by holding her over the stove. Sometime after the first three years or so they moved into a small two-bedroom home. There, my parents kept rabbits, which my father would slaughter for food. The basement, with its wooden walls and dirt floor, served as a root cellar.

My father's employment during these first five years was sketchy. One of his employers regularly lacked sufficient funds to pay his workers; as the word got out to businesses and stores in my parents' part of town, my mother would find herself walking the wooden sidewalks looking for an establishment that would agree to cash my father's paychecks. For a while my father took on a job as an orderly at a local mental hospital, where he was given odd jobs to do, including, one afternoon, the task of sewing closed the chest cavity of a body after an autopsy had been completed, the doctor in charge suddenly having to leave. And then there was a period of unemployment, which my parents disrupted by selling the lot next to their tiny home and using the money for a stay of several months with family back in the Netherlands. Once regular work arrived, it created its own problems. My father helped to construct pulp mills in the isolated towns of Grande Prairie and Hinton, places eight and five hours away by car. With a friend he would drive home on Friday evenings through whatever weather Alberta would throw at them, and make the return trip late Sunday afternoons, leaving my mother alone, in a strange land, with their children for another week. Near the end of her life my mother would occasionally tell me and others, in the presence of my father (who would look away), that several times she thought it was all too hard, and that she should leave him. These are not the anecdotes my parents would dwell on while telling nostalgic stories of early life in Canada.

At any rate, the distractions of setting up a new life were so strenuous and absorbing that one didn't have the luxury of meditating on the War. Moreover, my parents had landed in an extended and supportive Dutch immigrant community, which at times shared food, assisted in finding work and in negotiating health care, and swapped stories of battles with the

English language. My parents formed intense friendships with others during this time, based on living through these struggles. We children knew many of these immigrants not by their surnames, but as Oom and Tante – Uncles and Aunts, for better or worse. A kind of forced kinship, there being no other family on this side of the ocean. The community was so self-enclosed, so totally self-sufficient, that until I was in my early teens I was not really aware my mother had an accent, an accent so thick that my daughter-in-law, born and raised in Nova Scotia, can't understand her when she speaks on the telephone.

Our particular immigrant community defined itself by religious affiliation, specifically our branch of the Dutch Calvinist tradition. Its boundaries were not porous. I did not know any Catholic Dutch immigrants, let alone immigrants unconnected to any faith. As for the large Ukrainian community in our part of town, they were completely unknown, mysterious. On an entirely different plane were those we called "Canadians," non-immigrants, with British names, and unchurched as far as we knew. Their daughters used lipstick and wore miniskirts. For a young person to date a Canadian was a sign they weren't taking their faith seriously, that they were now "backsliding," having taken up with an "outsider." Our community was not focused on integration, but on maintaining separation, and building its own institutions. Ours was an unacknowledged mix of religion and culture, and it saw no need to disentangle the two. But it took its faith seriously: building and establishing Christian schools populated entirely by Dutch immigrant children, and whose tuition could cost parents more than a third of a family's take-home pay. Our community also built a church building together, and in that building set up its own extracurricular activities. For boys, there was something called the Calvinist Cadet

Corps, with uniforms, badges to be earned, loyalty pledges to recite, and a roll call. Girls were Calvinettes. Yes, they were. The community was supportive, protective, and a little smug.

In Canada my parents found their own, not just in ethnicity and religion, but also in class. My father, an electrician, had a twelfth-grade education from a vocational school, and my mother left school in eighth grade to find work and support her widowed mother. My parents' connections in their new country were all working class, and we lived in Beverly, a working-class neighbourhood of Edmonton. The tonier Dutch immigrants tended to house themselves on the other side of town. All the houses were one-story bungalows – on the main floor a living room, kitchen, bathroom, and two bedrooms. I had a bedroom on the main floor; my brother had a bedroom to himself in the basement, and my two sisters shared a room in the basement as well, sometimes peaceably. We lived near the edge of town, a short drive to the chemical factory where my father worked, and near the city dump, which for me was a sometimes-playground, and one occasion a source for a gift. I found the chrome side mirror of a 1962 Chevy Impala and, pleased by its aerodynamic shininess, wrapped it up for my mother and presented it to her on Mother's Day. I do not recall her reaction, or that I ever saw the mirror again.

Despite the tight embrace of our Dutch community, its activities and beliefs completely surrounding our daily lives, it reached only so far into our home; it did not reach into our living with the ash of Amersfoort. This we did alone. There was no shared suffering in our community, no models of behaviour for my father. Through some kind of unacknowledged osmosis, we eventually knew but didn't talk about that there were others who had endured similar experiences, including a pastor two hours' drive away who had also been in Amersfoort.

(Years later, in college, I lived in the same house as a son of that pastor. We were friends, but by then I had forgotten or buried that Amersfoort connection. Memory does what it wants to do.) We didn't seek them out, and they left us alone. As it must have been for families of collaborators, who had also put an ocean between themselves and the War, we were alone in this. And in our home we did not share the solitude with each other. We did not talk about Amersfoort, in a general way, as a family. We never had the "so this is what is happening when Dad cries, and here's how you deal with it" talk.

Of course, our house was not silent, including about the past. Like all immigrants, my parents would reminisce about the old country (which they called "the old country," without irony, perhaps the last people in the world to do so). They always reminisced in Dutch, a language that I didn't usually register as a second language but was just part of the soup I swam in. Their use of Dutch on these occasions probably had something to do with their emotional connection to these memories, separated from their new life in Canada. No doubt burnished by nostalgia, these were always pleasant stories about the Netherlands and its superior cheeses, pranks my father had played as a child, the glories of fresh fish, and short glimpses into my mother's tempestuous home life. In the face of these reminiscences, as a young adult I once remarked to my mother that when I was very young I had conflated Holland with heaven. She laughed. I did not, for years, ask why they had left this heaven. It also took a while for me to notice, as I listened, that they divided these golden-hued reminiscences into two categories: "voor de oorlog" and "na de oorlog." Before the War, and after the War. There was no category called "oorlog." In place of that there was just an empty, silent space.

*

Dinner. Our kitchen, should it be recreated today, would be ironically vintage. It had square linoleum tiles on the floor, set in an alternating pattern; highly varnished cabinets in whose shine you could see the ghost of your face; formica counters and one of those formica kitchen tables with the legs that designers invariably set off at a slight angle from the table top – a dead giveaway, even should the formica be covered with a tablecloth, a thing which we rarely did because of spills. Preparations for dinner set off what always was a noisy time, beginning with the timeless squabbling over whose turn it was to set the table. (My oldest sister kept in her head a schedule for this and for doing the dishes. I was suspicious.) Dishes were taken down with a lot of clattering, and after rustling through the cutlery drawer there was not much care over what side of the plate the knives and forks went. Often my father would have to be called to the table, having been lying down before supper. Unlike the yelling we did to call in siblings from outside, rousing my father was done quietly, always by my mother.

Once world explorers and central to the spice trade, the Dutch did not use their advantage to develop an inventive cuisine. Our dinners would typically consist of a well-done roast, cooked in a Dutch oven; lots of yellow potatoes and gravy; and a mushy vegetable, often endive laced with nutmeg – a complicated and bitter taste that to this day I cannot abide. Always the nutmeg, a residue of Dutch colonialism that sprinkled down onto every mercilessly boiled vegetable. If the meal didn't begin with soup, dessert was implied, maybe "dead fly pudding" – custard with raisins embedded in it, and sometimes, in season, topped with deep purple saskatoon-berry sauce, made from berries we had picked from bushes in the river valley while warding off battalions of angry mosquitoes.

We settled down for the opening prayer. Every evening, my father began the meal with the Lord's Prayer, his intonation rising and falling in exactly the same places, with the same pacing, night after night, year after year, predictable, bounded, as warm and comfortable as the gravy on our potatoes. And then, in a rising voice, he said the Amen, after which the noise would return, like that of starlings on a bird feeder. Some hysterical laughter, which at times would erupt again at the closing Bible reading time, when my father, unable to control his own laughter, wouldn't be able to finish the passage, and set the Bible aside, shaking his head, abashed but not upset. My mother would be unamused, but I loved it – because of the triumph of my and my siblings' anarchic wit, because my friends' fathers rarely laughed, and perhaps because it held something else at bay. Dinner was done when all the endive was eaten, or threatened to be set aside for my breakfast, supposedly before I would get anything else.

And then, every night, for all the years of my childhood, inevitably, tension would build, our communal ease would end, and we would each enter into our loneliness. I knew what was coming. Suspicious of anything that had the odour of Catholic or Anglican liturgy and pomp, Dutch Calvinists believed they had few religious rituals, few times when things are preordained as to how they will go, that proceed predictably once they begin to unfold. But in their religious practices they did tend to do the same things the same way, every day. In our home, dinner-time devotions were that kind of daily ritual. It was a ritual in which time stopped and put focus on our day. At the end of the meal my father would reach to a drawer and take the Bible out for closing devotions. Over time he would read through the Bible in order and then start from the beginning again, although after a few days of trying he usually gave up on reading us through the longer genealogies or the book of Leviticus, with its endless ceremonial regulations ("the rock badger, because it chews the cud but does not part the hoof, is unclean to you").

Endless genealogies of "begats" or tedious passages of ceremonial law, though, at least had their calming effects – on those nights we knew there would be no trouble. But Bible reading was rarely a restful time; Amersfoort was always ready to step in and set our family ritual off in an agonizing direction, a direction we set out on or anticipated nightly. Any passage, anything, could send my father and us off. This was particularly true when he read passages that touched on God's grace and steadfastness, especially those passages that touched on suffering and death, or on God's leading through times of trouble. Psalm 69, for example, can stand in for how things went on those nights. Pausing and clearing his throat, my father began his reading confidently, although this particular passage signalled danger right from the beginning:

> Save me, O God!
> For the waters have come up to my neck.
> I sink in deep mire,

And then he would pause, as if his vision had blurred and he was trying to make out the next words. The pause went on longer than a momentary loss of focus required, and in that silent gap all restless movement around the table stopped and, as one, our family started to look down. My breathing tightened. I knew where we were headed, that our own private ritual was unfolding as it always did, and that there was no stopping it, and no opting out. Taking a breath, my father would start in again:

> where there is no foothold;
> I have come into deep waters,

Another, longer pause, and now I could feel the table start to shake. My hands and chest would tighten, and with my jaw clenching I would try to silently *will* him through whatever this was. I wasn't listening to God's word, I wasn't cheering him on, I just wanted it to end. A few more words, wavering pauses between them now:

> and the flood sweeps over me.
> I am weary . . . with my crying;
> . . . my throat is . . . parched.

Another pause, and he would circle back a few words, taking a run at them, trying to force them to come out right this time, or maybe building up impetus so that he could push past what was coming:

> . . . my throat is parched.
> My eyes grow dim
> with waiting for my God.

Whatever it was for him, for me the Bible reading became an endurance test of waiting in a familiar place, trapped, in the presence of my father, forced to endure his trauma, unable to move or blink, unable to understand why this was happening, watching him, through his increasingly long and tremulous pauses, through his returning to an interrupted phrase, his bearing down and straining to compel the words to come out properly, with heavy sighs and stifled sniffing, waiting for his inevitable and shameful defeat:

> More in number than the hairs of my head
> are those who hate me . . . without cause;
> mighty . . . are those who would . . . destroy me,

And then, with short, jagged sobs he would put the book down, still opened in his hands, and look away. No one spoke or looked up in the ensuing silence. My mother would quietly take the open Bible from my father's hands and pass it to my brother. With her flat, determined voice, she would say: "Bill, you take over." (My father never resisted at this point; passive, he had stopped being an agent in this ritual.) And Bill, in this composite memory maybe fourteen or fifteen years old, would have to finish. I felt sorry for him but wasn't sure why. It just didn't seem right.

We couldn't just walk away at this point; our family ritual had a few more steps to be endured. No matter how disastrous the Bible reading had been, the closing prayer was non-negotiable. Even when, at times, my father made it through the Bible reading and then went on to the closing prayer, at that point I, hearing him begin, would feel the same anxieties rise. Unlike those of other fathers, his closing prayers were neither formulaic nor short. Relatives in the Netherlands and their difficulties were enumerated, petitions made for the poor and sick, prayers given for the church across the world and for those being persecuted. (The closing prayer was called "giving thanks," but my father's prayers, dealing with the uncertainties and troubles of the world, was more mournful than thankful.) But if my father had been having a bad day, he would not get through his prayer, and would break off, wavering, pausing, and then crying, before the end.

Again, in our family setting there was nothing to do about it when you saw it coming; once he began praying you didn't intervene. You were strapped in, unable to move out of it. There was no other choice. In all the years in which we regularly restaged this ritual, no one ever left the table, or said anything. No children cried or made a fuss. So, I and the rest of the family would just stand aside and once again wait out a slow-moving train wreck.

My witnessing of his collapse, however, was partial – I only heard what was happening. I kept my eyes shut, but not out of piety. (Piety was not my long suit. At times during prayer when he was clearly *not* struggling with his emotions, I would make faces at my sisters to get them to laugh and be in trouble.) But I almost never opened my eyes when the crying started. I would squeeze them tighter, not wanting to see something so horrible – my father, alone, gripped by something malevolent, with nothing to be done, either by him or us. But at rare times I couldn't help myself, and I did something that felt disrespectful. Propelled by some weird inner force, I would briefly lift my head, open my eyes slightly, and through the filter of my eyelashes see something that at the time I felt was both heroic and shameful – my father, his head and folded hands trembling, tears streaming down his cheeks, stammering out some kind of prayer to God, some kind of asking for mercy and relief for others, but not for himself, never for himself. Then I would shut my eyes again.

While the ending prayer was non-negotiable, my father wasn't always the one to do it. If the Bible reading had been particularly difficult that evening, my mother would head things off before the prayer and quietly say, without looking at my father or at us, "I will pray." Again, the flat, determined voice. (Her taking on this role, I knew, was big in some way

I didn't understand. Women never prayed aloud in our community, but my mother was no ordinary woman.) After the prayer my father would reach into his pocket, take out his hankie, blow his nose, and then leave the table silently and go, alone, eyes downcast, to his bedroom, close the door, and lie down. No one acknowledged what had happened or comforted him. He didn't look at us, and we didn't look at him or at each other. Our bodies gradually unstiffening, we left our solitude and turned back to regular life, going outside to play, or squabbling over whose turn it was to do the dishes. This is what normal people do.

Both my father's struggles and their emotional impact on me remain vivid. More than fifty years later I can still see it in all its details and feel its imprint, my jaw once again clenching, my gut tightening, my heart beginning to race. Years later, trying to parse these horrible moments, I remember the weights of his pauses caused me more anxiety than did his crying. It was the terrible silence in the pauses of my father's devotions, bottomless silence, unbearable. During those wordless moments when he found himself unable to speak, time stopped. Everything was teetering, waiting to crash, but we all had to dangle just a little bit longer, waiting. Certainly the crying that followed was difficult, but at least once my father began to cry you knew today's ritual was ending. In those intense moments of silence, pressing on me like a vise, my father and I were pulling in opposite directions, and I could not follow him, where he was going.

My father's determination to undergo this awful dinner ritual was and still is inexplicable to me. Rituals are performative acts; they are supposed to *do* something. It's unclear to me what our family devotions *did*, other than raise my anxiety to an excruciating level. And my father's motivations for insisting on his particular manner of enacting our ritual is still unclear. He was in charge of it; he chose to put his trauma on display for us, day after day. Sure, devotions were non-negotiable in our culture, although its functions weren't always obvious. And my father had an over-developed sense of obligation: he did things because they were the things that were done, and people were counting on him to do those things. Perhaps in our family ritual he was simply trying to be a good father, doing what every father in our circle did, leading in family devotions. Perhaps. But why so dogged in trying to read through those difficult passages – the Bible has its happy and blessed moments too, after all. He could have worked at decreasing the odds of breaking down. And why, knowing he was about to cry, why didn't he just *stop*, why, every time, did he try to continue, to impose his will on his trauma, and in so doing torture himself and us? Did he think that just this one night he would be able to pull it off? I don't know what was being proved, or for whom, whether this was a private struggle with God or himself when his trauma bore down on him, or whether he was aware of his family, and trying to do something for them. If the latter, his only clear acknowledgement of us through this excruciating process was at the end, when he avoided eye contact and walked away to be by himself. And that moment was filled with an ambiguity I still don't understand. Those averted eyes, what did they signify? Fatigue? Shame? Defeat? How far did his emotions – whatever they were – extend? Where were we in his mind, if at all?

I was never sure what I was supposed to take away from watching and enduring this mix of panic, anger, agony, and God knows what else. On a primal level I just didn't want to be there. It wasn't that these devotions created a spiritual crisis for me, as a child. I wasn't particularly thinking about God during these stressful times; I was thinking about my father and hoping "this" would all end soon – and the "this" referred to the experience, not its theological implications, whatever those might be. My anxiety was tied up with the inevitable, inescapable rhythm of the experience. I hated it, but there was nothing I could do about it. I knew every move of this awful dance, could predict each ungainly step – my fear wasn't like the experience of a sudden unknown, terrifying event, such as suddenly finding yourself face to face with some stranger who wanted to hurt you. Actually, I wasn't face to face with anybody. My father during these times was out of reach – he wasn't communicating with me, but with himself, and maybe with God. All through dinner my father had been there, and now, at a time that was solemn and important in our family, he wasn't anymore, and I wasn't sure why, or where he was. I knew I couldn't ask, and I also knew that in some fundamental way I was on my own, and not just during devotions.

Yet while these mealtime rituals were difficult to get through, as a child I never thought of them as strange; I didn't think in terms of whether my life was normal or not. It just *was*. My father's crying, my mother's grim interventions, and our silent relationship to it all was a pattern whose contours we knew in advance, a recurrent set of volatile actions in whose wake we acted as if nothing strange had happened. The experience of it was a solitary one of watching, quiet and evasive – none of us children later whispered to each other, "What's up with Dad?" (The silence was powerful and long in its reach: these bouts of crying in front of the family occurred regularly in the years before the car incident, the incident in which I first shamefully broke the silence, and continued years after that, until he was no longer able to read because of his failing eyesight.) In the silence, perhaps because of the silence, all I could do was watch, hoping – *willing* – it to end, for some reason neither fight nor flight being available options. The watching was so visceral for me that, as a young boy, I didn't even try to interpret what was happening. It was too confusing and intense. To be sure, it wasn't our whole day or our whole lives together. Not everything was taken over by Amersfoort – but it regularly sifted down around us, reorienting things, putting them back in place.

My Secret Life

OCCASIONALLY my mother would take me along on a visit to Tante Aafke, her friend from church. We would enter the house, and I would immediately smell both strong coffee and old cigars – Tante Aafke's husband, Gerrit, trailed clouds of cigar smoke wherever he went. The ash went everywhere, even into his unpopular oliebollen (traditional deep-fried fritters) he made every New Year's Day and served after the church service that morning. I wasn't offered coffee, but I did get a piece of cake with a tiny fork, the size of the fork indicating this was an occasion. And then I was directed to the toy closet at the end of a hall to spend the rest of our time, while my mother and Tante Aafke chatted. Inside the closet were stacks and stacks of comic books, including a pile of Stan Lee *Sgt. Fury and his Howling Commandos* comics, undoubtedly the property of Bruce, Tante Aafke's son, a boy about four years older than I. Sergeant Fury, heroic and alarming, fought his way through Nazi Europe, breaking the teeth and shooting through the torsos of multiple Prussian SS men, some with the *de rigueur* dueling scar on the cheek, and maybe even an eye patch. Sitting not in a chair, but hunkered down on the broadloom carpet, I gulped the comics down in big batches, as fast as I could, my face in a corner and *Sgt. Fury* nestled inside a harmless *Archie* comic, which I used as a cover. Maybe eight or nine years old at the time, I didn't know anything about Amersfoort, but I did know I had to hide this tasty and shameful activity.

It wasn't the only thing. When at the age of eight I was hospitalized for an appendectomy and my parents had gone home for the day, I begged the nurses to allow me to stay up late to watch, with the older children, the characters of *The Rat Patrol* careen through the North African desert in their machine-gun mounted jeeps, blasting their way through Field Marshall Rommel's Afrika Korps, Rommel's exploding jeeps and soldiers flying through the air. And, later, I enjoyed the breathtaking inanities of *Hogan's Heroes*, of wide-eyed Sergeant Schultz stammering "I see nothing!", watching with my brother in his basement bedroom, switching the channel when my father checked in to see what we were doing, silently standing in the doorway, perhaps suspecting what we were up to but saying nothing. And I, like some other boys in my immigrant school, drew swastikas on my pink eraser, and, using partially embedded staples as caterpillar track, pretended it was a tank fighting its way across the Western Europe of my desktop as the school day crept on.

I can recreate for myself, even at a remove of more than fifty years, what the furtive experience of doing these things felt like, but I don't know why I did them. I do know that I sensed these activities were a little shameful, and that after a time they became impossible, all without ever reasoning my way through or talking about it. It was the family way. Sure, I was a child, but a child knows things.

Mom

A FEW YEARS AGO, when my mother was in her mid-nineties, I called my parents at their rest home in Surrey, British Columbia. My father answered, a little distracted. In place of the normal silence of their apartment, in the background I could hear the repeated sounds of something being torn. After a few sentences he handed me off to my mother, who came on and began speaking in her unique tone of evasion, a tone both briskly cheerful and matter-of-fact, a tone indicating that, while she might talk to me, she could not be touched. She was, she informed me, ripping up her war diary. "Yes," she said, "I was just reading a part where we were headed for the safest place in our home because the German V-2 bombs were falling again." (Her wartime home had been near the launching pad of these experimental and famously unstable weapons.) My reaction was physical, panicked, but in the face of my spluttering she calmly listed her reasons for destroying her diary: the diary is in Dutch, she said, which nobody can read anymore; nobody remembers this time; and besides, all the people it refers to are dead now. Nobody knows them. What is the use of keeping it, another thing which we children would then be stuck with cleaning up after she died? After I began protesting that I could read Dutch, that I wanted to know what had happened to her during the War, and that it was precisely because nobody could remember that time anymore that the diary was important, she abruptly ended the conversation, handed the phone back to my father, and by the sounds of things returned to complete her work.

And so, my mother once again policed the boundaries of what would be known about the War. Upset, I called my brother to tell him what had just happened. He was stunned, and not just because she was destroying her diary. Neither of us knew that she even had a war diary. She had never alluded to it during the more than seventy years since the end of the War. If we had known of its existence, and suspected she wanted to destroy it, we agreed we would have taken it long ago. That bit of ineffectual bravado doesn't bear ethical scrutiny, but it does reveal our need to latch on to something that could help us understand who she was, why she behaved the way she did, what was behind her silence and her abrupt way of managing my father's regular eruptions of Amersfoort. Ripping up her diary was baffling, a performative gesture that aggressively closed off that part of her past from us and perhaps from herself – although what it meant for her we would never know.

As the destruction of her diary suggests, my mother was not just a force for controlling how our family saw and understood my father's trauma, for how we were schooled to behave in the face of his emotional extravagance, how we froze or tiptoed around it, eyes averted – no questions, no digging, just move on – she was also parsimonious in doling out stories from her own past. It was all of one piece. The stories from her past were few, and when she told them they were never fleshed out, their significance unclear. Her stories had no larger meaning, the way my father's War was always a story about God's care. When dealing with seemingly difficult material she did not help her children think through what it might have meant to her or what they could mean to us. They always ended quickly, and she brusquely moved on to a new topic and a different tone, usually lighthearted. No questions allowed.

Her childhood, what I know of it, was not easy. Her father was a fisherman, and the family sold fish door to door, from a dog cart in the early years. Sometime before she was born they moved from the fishing village of Scheveningen, across the city of The Hague, to Loosduinen, far from the rowdiness and pungency of Scheveningen harbor. In Loosduinen they were at the bottom of the social ladder, teased for the smell of fish reputed to cling to them. After her father's death, my mother and grandmother became reliant on the benevolence of the church, and after eighth grade my mother needed to quit school to work in a store. She never presented this change as a disappointment, a closing off of opportunity. It was what was needed, so you did it. By my mother's telling, her mother was depressed for years, until her death soon after the War, when my mother was in her early twenties. My mother occasionally gave glimpses into a home life that was tempestuous and at times angry – she recalled her mother thrusting a scalding hot boiled potato into her brother's mouth to stop him from talking. When provoked, my mother reverted to the salty vocabulary of her upbringing. Her expressions were always in Dutch, whose lexicon, she insisted, was more genteel than the English equivalents I occasionally let fly at home (flying in the face of all evidence, as I rapidly found out during a visit to the Netherlands when I was sixteen and tried out my inherited Dutch vocabulary on my unamused oma). She wouldn't tolerate even the mildest English swearing, let alone manage to pronounce it properly.

Until the very end of her life my mother shared very little of her time during the War. What I learned, I learned casually, from snippets disbursed in side comments and never presented as trauma, anecdotes which ultimately I could connect together only by virtue of them all having happened to her. In what must have been a difficult decision for the family, her older nephew and one of her brothers were conscripted – and complied – to do the kind of work for the Nazis that my father was imprisoned for attempting to avoid. Near the end of the War, she and her mother ate a cat to stay alive. And, of course, she tried to hide from falling V-2 rockets, a detail I learned completely by accident, a detail whose revealing was preceded by the sounds of ripping paper.

She occasionally told her startled children and grandchildren a story of having stayed at a friend's house past curfew and needing to return home. The friend's father volunteered to escort her on this risky journey, in blackout darkness, hiding from any German soldiers who might be patrolling. They made it. And then on her doorstep her friend's father grabbed and kissed her, deeply and long. My mother told us that she thought, "Well, nothing much is happening anyway these days, so I might as well." And she kissed him back. As with many of her stories, the purpose of the telling was unclear, and her attitude unsettling. My only clear takeaway from this particular anecdote is that after telling it she always had a quiet smile on her face.

To her listeners, these anecdotes often felt like an afterthought. About ten years ago, while drinking coffee with my mother, I asked her to fill me in on the story of her brother, my Oom Arie, who soon after the War moved to Norway with his wife, my Tante Solveig. Tante Solveig was Norwegian, so the move made some kind of sense, but internally I had been wondering whether it was because Oom Arie had had an experience similar to my father, or whether he had been a collaborator. Casually, over coffee and cake, I pressed a bit. While in a later conversation I learned that they moved because Tante Solveig was terribly unhappy in her new country, that afternoon I learned something different. As was my mother's way, she didn't so much answer my questions as take the conversation in an unexpected direction:

> Tante Solveig was not Oom Arie's first wife. At the start of the War he was married to a different woman, and they adopted a beautiful little boy with curly hair. The cutest boy. But during the War she took up with a German soldier, and when the War ended the people in Scheveningen shaved her head, paraded her through the street, ran her out of town, and we never saw her or the boy with the curly hair again. Can I have another piece of cake?

And then she picked up her fork, contentedly tucked into her second piece of cake and didn't speak again, while I looked on, aghast. (Oom Arie's children only found out about this story well after his death, around 2010 or so, as a result of a chance comment by my mother. Initially baffled and angry at the family secrecy, as I understand it they did search for and eventually find the boy with the curly hair.)

It was a typical story for her, both in its content and how it was presented. My mother told all the stories about her past in a flat, matter-of-fact tone, and from my point of view with little attention to crafting. (The collaborating wife narrative could have used some work on pacing and suspense, and some decent denouement. On the other hand, if her intent was to leave me bewildered and gasping, she succeeded.) For all the stories from her past, my mother controlled when they were presented, and how they ended. Once she reached for the cake, one couldn't probe, or ask follow-up questions. Her stories stopped, but they didn't conclude. And her war stories never had much of a point – they just *were*, they abruptly surfaced and then disappeared beneath the waves again. They offered glimpses, but not much self-revelation. Despite her stories, she was alone with her past, and she wanted it that way. And she applied that way of dealing with one's past to my father, upset by his physical expressions of his trauma, and neither approving of nor understanding his eventual need, in the ending decades of his life, to speak of Amersfoort.

It is no surprise, then, that over the years I sensed there were stories she didn't tell, things that had happened to her other than the few she was willing to speak of, things that had affected her deeply, and which she would only obliquely allude to – just that some things had happened to her. She was the only one who knew the weight of them, but occasionally I caught glimpses. About a half year after my father died, my mother interrupted her usual monologue to me on the phone – a monologue detailing the inadequate attention my sister gave her, the sketchy way she had landed in nursing care, and her wish to die that evening – with some of her thinking about the afterlife. She wondered whether the Bible's promise of a new earth and heaven was for a literally different place or not, and how that all might work. And then my mother said she hoped she would not recognize anyone in heaven, not even her children and her husband. She did not want to recognize anyone, she said, because that would mean she would also remember her life on earth, and there were some memories she wanted obliterated. In exchange for the disappearance of the difficult things in her life, she was willing also to delete her memories of the people who had loved her.

A few weeks after that call, I visited my mother again. She had turned one hundred just a few months before, and was often tired and having difficulty coping. I visited her twice a day, usually for a little under two hours, and as always, she did the talking. She wasn't all that happy, and each time unfurled her litany of complaints, about the staff, about my sister, about the food, about how she had been exiled from my father. To some degree I didn't blame her, one hundred years of age, everything hurting, tired all the time, not being able to see very much, and suspecting that her mind was starting to slip. Her mind moved around a lot, swooping from topic to topic, and, increasingly, into the distant past, to places she had never spoken about. Now with my father gone she began to talk about the War – her War, not my father's – a time that over several visits she described as five years of "vervelende dingen" (nasty things).

And so one morning I made the short walk from my sister's house to her nursing home, punched in the code to the building and then to the elevator, walked through the communal area where I was greeted either with unseeing stares or a friendly wave, and arrived at her room, with the clock she could no longer see; the electric scooter being charged up for the day's activities; the table crowded with half-full juice glasses, cards, and tissues; and on the wall the framed photograph and congratulatory letter from King Charles and Queen Camilla, congratulating her on turning one hundred.

As one often found her now, my mother was lying in bed, tired and upset about some disagreement she had had at the start of her day. After walking me through that, she began to talk, with only my murmurs and an occasional question signalling that this was kind of a conversation. As she spoke, she lay on her side facing me with her eyes closed, under a blanket, one hand cupped under her head, and her free hand stroking a pillow. Her talking and anecdotes went back and forth, her tone never changing while her speech shuttled seamlessly between English and Dutch, wandering between the far and near past without distinguishing much between the two. It was going to be one of her epic talks – this time for an hour and a half without a break – and, as always when she got going, with her eyes closed. Her shutting her eyes meant something; it closed off any chance at interchange with anyone in the room, any openings for comment or empathy, for explorations of what things meant for her or for her listeners. The past was being recounted but not reopened. This was a closed event.

She began by briefly referring to what she saw as the thirty good years she had had with my father, the years beginning in middle age, years of contentment and travel, punctuating that with a reference to the difficulty of the War. To my occasional brief prompts over the next half hour she began to speak with a level of detail I had never witnessed, and told stories I had never heard of before. The Hunger Winter was hard, she said, "Ja, terrible. We were bombed, but near us, not on us. It could happen at any moment.... Je zit er midden in" (you are stuck in the middle of it). She said that during the War she and her mother lived in dirty circumstances – a poorly constructed home, right next to a dirty ditch filled with garbage. It was "smerig" (dirty, nasty), she said, grimacing slightly. Her talk then shifted to a different time, to her pleasure at seeing how her children had turned out, then to her father's taste for pork and the possible connection of that to his death from an infected boil, and finally to her pleasure in making bacon and eggs for my father on Saturday mornings.

And then she turned back to the War: "It was okay; we were free. But scary. As soon as we heard an airplane we were scared. They were very close." Despite the fear she had to go on with her daily life, twenty minutes of cycling alone along the Haagweg to get to her job. When I asked if there were soldiers around, she said there were a few, at checkpoints, where they would have to feel what she was carrying in her bags.

And then, except for an occasional murmur, she circled around an event – getting near, pulling back, and approaching it again, her speech more and more settling into Dutch: "The best food went to the soldiers. We got what was left. We had vegetables and occasionally a little rabbit to eat. Rabbit meat was tasty, but it didn't happen often . . . For the teenagers it was worse. Well, if you were sixteen you had to go to Germany to work or to fight. And I was just sixteen . . . They decided they needed to squeeze my breasts." She stumbled over her words and then chuckled, quoting a soldier: "Does your boyfriend do this, too?" and continued, "Ja, I let him just go, but I thought if you go too far I will start to kick. He had to feel me, just because he could, because he could do it . . . Hij was . . . En ik, ja . . .

"I needed to get wood. There were houses along the Kijkduinsestraat, by the North Sea. The houses were made of wood and were all empty. We went there for the kitchens, which we broke down. Well, not me, but the men, and then the women would have to transport it, what the men had left behind and what they could not use. The men would go out at night, and then we went at three in the morning to these North Sea houses, in the dark, to get the wood. I was sixteen . . . If you were lucky, you didn't encounter anyone because they were all fighting. But there was always one. When I got there the others had already been there, secretly, to get the wood. But I was alone with my bike. So I couldn't run, I couldn't ride my bike, I had to walk next to it. And so they could just grab me. . . . Ja . . . Well, if it had just been that he had stopped me, but ja . . . Look. I was alone, I was a girl. And he could tease and torment me and do things. But you had to watch out, because these Germans went out with local girls . . . But good. I stood there alone with the German. I needed myself to remain calm, because if I had gotten angry it would have ended differently, of course. So I let him go on, until finally he let me go . . . But you don't forget these things.

"And there were quite a few girls who wanted a little fun and went out with the Germans and who were later punished, shaved bald." She chuckled ruefully. "Hair is so important." She paused, straightened herself, sat up a bit, took a sip of her coffee, and without missing a beat changed directions. "But we always had good friends. I worked in the milk store. I became wise, it was a big operation." And then to immigrant life: "You did what you could with each other. And then Oom Bert, a good man."

And she was off again, in yet a new direction, the War behind her, sort of. This was my mother. This was the woman who ripped up her war diary and wanted her memory erased in heaven. I don't know what to make of her story, a story she told in a flat voice, at a single unhurried pace, and from which she moved away quickly. There is so much silence here. The purposes of her telling were unclear. The flatness meant something, and it had an effect on me, but what it meant to her, I don't know. She didn't seem to tell her story to help me understand who she was, or to elicit my sympathy – she didn't look at me while speaking, or pause for me to comment. She didn't provide any of her own commentary, how it had shaped her, how it had damaged her, or maybe how she had come out on the other side okay. Though my father's death seems to have freed her to tell it, what it meant to her is private, like most of her stories. I don't know what to do with it, the flatness of her tone, how to have it sit in my body.

Of all her stories, there was only one from her life that she wanted her children to understand as traumatic, a story that she told several times, a story about the night her father died. The youngest child by ten years in her family at the time of her father's death, she was the only child at home. Her father had suffered from an infection that began from a boil on his neck, a condition that had worsened. The final crisis came in the middle of the night, and he was rushed to the hospital. My mother, an eight-year-old child, was left behind, sleeping, alone. The next-door neighbour had been alerted and agreed to come early in the morning to wake my mother and feed her breakfast. But instead of sleeping through, my mother woke up in the middle of the night to discover the silent house empty. Alone in the dark, with no one to hear, she screamed and screamed. That is where she always ended her story – not with people rushing in to comfort her later, or with what she felt at the death of her father, but of her being alone in the house and the world, with no one to hear her terror. When she told us this story, it was clear this was not one of her matter-of-fact anecdotes, told casually, off the cuff, but something bigger, more haunting. This was a story with a purpose, a story about a little girl abandoned, a story at times told with laboured breathing near its end. But she always closed it off from us, inviting neither comment nor sympathy, and would steer us in a new direction.

*

After the War, my mother began a new life with my father. Four years older than he, she had known him at a distance for years, and has alluded to triumphing over the competition, an acquaintance whom she shouldered aside and she steered towards a lesser cousin of my father. There were several key "na de oorlog" stories of their courtship: canoeing, picnicking together unsupervised, a marriage proposal, losing and then finding her engagement ring on a beach, and how, soon after the War, my father spent much of his weekly wages to buy my mother the gift of a bunch of rare but slightly overripe bananas. That last, she said, was one of the most romantic gestures of her life. And so, they married. He was handsome and funny, she was beautiful, lively, and practical, someone who could push things aside and make things work. They married despite their social differences, differences felt keenly by my father's parents. Oma let her disapproval of my mother's origins be known. In contrast to my mother's fishing heritage, my father's family was a few nuanced steps higher up Loosduinen's social ladder: his father was a psychiatric nurse, and his mother prided herself on being the daughter of a well-known tailor who had customers among the Dutch nobility. They were not high society, but higher than some, and always clarified that boundary by reaching up – with greasy gestures like asking my father to hand-deliver a congratulatory card to Loosduinen's mayor on his birthday, a story my father told me, in distaste and with a grimace, as in his closing years he revaluated his life with them.

My mother had her eyes open to those differences. In her nineties, frustrated with the increasing speed and drama of my father's downward spiral deeper into his trauma, and eager to point out how hard he had become to live with, she told me of her mother-in-law's own sense of how Amersfoort had impacted him, and the practical consequences: "Oma allowed me to marry Dad because he was damaged goods."

I stopped breathing and looked down. She said it cruelly, matter-of-factly, and then, as was her way, turned to other things.

Other than the occasions when my father's trauma erupted, during my childhood my mother most often was a happy woman. I can see and hear her singing hymns while hanging out the laundry on a crystal-clear but freezing Edmonton winter day, belting out the chorus:

> Whiter than snow, yes, whiter than snow
> Now wash me and I shall be
> Whiter than snow.

And then later she would exuberantly run in with the freeze-dried bedsheets, stiff as boards, and compel me to sample how heavenly they smelled. Not as openly religious as my father, she particularly enjoyed her own set of tacky Dutch post-war songs, many featuring rambunctious if ethically iffy seductions. One, about Trees, a young Dutch woman whose rudimentary English only contains affirmatives and who falls for a liberating Canadian soldier, is the most persistent ear-worm on my vast playlist:

> Trees heeft een Canadees
> O wat is dat kindje in d'r sas
> Trees heeft een Canadees
> Samen in de Jeep en dan vol gas.

> (Trees has got herself a Canadian
> Oh, she's having a great time
> Trees has got herself a Canadian
> Together in the Jeep and then full gas.)

My mother relished the milder pleasures of the world: eating a meal outdoors, washing her feet in cold mountain streams, savouring a beautiful piece of smoked fish. She enjoyed mischief – in the kitchen, sneaking up behind someone with a wrapped piece of frozen meat for the evening meal in her hand, and pressing it against a warm and unsuspecting neck. If she handed me a banana for my lunch she would advance on me like a drunk gangster, pretending the banana was a gun, and making inaccurate shooting noises – "peef paf poof." In public, her happiness could be impulsive and unpredictable, seizing the joy of the moment to behave in ways that I found deeply embarrassing and which I now probably replicate. To my hissed teenage protests she would respond: "Nobody knows us here, and if they do – they understand." Her exuberance made my father happy, and she loved him. I am sure of that.

She loved and managed him and our home, filtering how we children interacted with and understood his trauma, wanting to keep us at bay from the specifics of what had happened. For the seventy-plus years of her marriage my mother saw herself as the one holding things together, and while she wasn't always pleased about that (family devotions made that clear), outside of those moments she was typically happy and loving to my father, and for years her strategies kept a lid on things, with some notable triumphs. Five years after moving to Canada she was the one who, despite my father's unemployment at the time, propelled my father and the rest of the family on a trip back to the Netherlands to visit her in-laws, as she had promised to our skeptical and dour oma. When I was in my early forties she learned that the German government was finally willing to pay reparations to those who had been incarcerated and forced to work.

My father, typically the passive one, resisted, saying the past was the past. She started the process, but there were other problems – the German government would pay reparations only to those whose papers were in order, and initially it seemed my father's were incomplete. My mother, with her eighth-grade education but her Scheveningen temperament, set her jaw and refused to alter course, eventually, after multiple letters, forcing bureaucracy to bend to her will. She, as she always did, persisted, even when it seemed a fool's errand or inappropriate. When we were awarded the restitution money (which my adolescent son called the Nazi Gold, a term which has stuck), my parents spent it on a huge party – a week-long family reunion at a resort in British Columbia, all expenses paid. It was not a week of talking through and coming to terms with my father's past – it was never going to be that – but something we were better at: a week of eating, of swimming, of stupid and fiercely competitive games, and of plastic water toys, including a giant octopus, in whose inflated arms we laughed and drank. And we watched my parents trying to work together to navigate a paddle boat, smiling and muttering instructions to each other, but only managing to go round and round in slow circles in shallow water, to shrieks of laughter from their children and grandchildren on shore. A kind of retort, on our part, to the past.

But my mother's joy was complicated, and over the years increasingly shaded off into something darker. During the early 1990s, when my parents and my mother's sister Tante Lien visited Susan and me in Nova Scotia, we took them out to the village of Terence Bay. It was a lovely sunny day, and there the two sisters found the community graveyard, a beautiful, overgrown rambly place, with paths meandering through waist-high vegetation, thick with the scent of wild roses and the requisite murmuring of hundreds of bees, and offering a stunning view of the bay and its islands. The cemetery was filled with the graves of the 535 people who had perished in the wreck of the ss *Atlantic*, an immigrant ship run aground in 1873. My father, Susan, and I soaked in the beauty, but my mother and her sister, wandering off by themselves, moved in a different direction and spent a contented hour ambling past the graves, deciding on which deaths had been terrible, which were not so terrible, and which were off-the-charts terrible ("erg," "niet zo erg," "hartstikke erg"). As far as I could tell, the rationale behind the ranking was based on the age of the deceased, whether other family members had also died, a stated or implied parental status, and the nuances that arose from the interaction of these factors. The ranking was complicated, clinical, and totally absorbing.

So despite or alongside her exuberant capacity for fun, my mother saw the world as an unstable place, full of misfortunes lurking around every corner, and when misfortunes did reveal themselves, they were to be enumerated, discussed, and appreciated for their nuances – a tendency that increased markedly as she aged, when her appetite for more traditional pleasures shrivelled and her focus narrowed. In the last decades of her life she increasingly occupied herself with telling and retelling the unfortunate stories not of my father, whose references to his time in Amersfoort had exhausted and frustrated her, but of the residents in her care home, or those of the extended families of her caregivers. It wasn't empathy. Savouring morose details was embedded in her constitution, a schadenfreude, an aesthetic pleasure that more and more filled her days.

The virtue my mother prided herself on the most was her practicality, a characteristic which pervaded everything

Little Shuswap Lake, British Columbia, 2006

she did, even if it meant, as it did near the end of her life, that a commode with its lid down made an adequate chair for guests (with a cushion, to be sure), and, should the need arise, a serviceable coffee table. Her practicality was so engrained she couldn't see outside of its confines, baffled why visitors balked at sitting on what was a perfectly fine chair, nice and high, easy to get in and out of, and with arms. She had no breath for things that did not have an immediate practical purpose. Most central to her life with my father was that she believed trauma, especially my father's trauma, had to be dealt with practically, so that life could go on. You set the Bible away, purse your lips, and get on with the evening's tasks. She believed, with my father's trauma, as with the commode, that she was simply being "realistic," a phrase she often used to shut down objections to her sometimes-inexplicable behaviours. She didn't dwell on the past, neither to emote nor as a form of therapy. Just look straight ahead. For her, emotions and empathy weren't practical, they muddled things. Silence, and turning to something else, was a better response. What she modelled and what we learned from her was how to shut down when my father's trauma became too much, how to become flat and just get through it. And for a while it could seem, if you looked at her brand of practicality, how she responded in the face of an erupting trauma – if you looked at it in terms of getting through the day in front of you, and in just the right light, from the perfect angle, and not for too long, that just maybe she might be right.

Religion and Faith

SUNDAY MORNING after breakfast we put on our church clothes: good pants and a nice cotton shirt with buttons for me, a suit and tie for my father, a hat and full dress for my mother. No sport coats, no skirts for them. My father was always impatient to get to church on time, and "on time" meant being in our pew at least fifteen minutes before the service began, well before the organ prelude started. (There was an early and a late service. We always went to the early one and suspected those who attended the 11:00 a.m. service of being a little less serious, even to the point of their probably being "oncers," not attending the late afternoon service.) We packed into our white 1963 Chevrolet BelAir, drove the mile to church, parked, climbed the high, wide stairs, and entered the building.

The church, built by members of the congregation, was undecorated inside, with standard wooden pews arranged in a T; a pipe organ taking up a lot of space in the balcony; and a pulpit, front, centre, and high. (The pulpit was the centre of the church service. From that height the long sermon would be given by the minister, whom all the adults called "dominee," or "lord.") We settled into our pew. It wasn't official, but everyone headed to the same place every Sunday, like cows, each to their own designated milking stall. Some of the older teenagers got to sit with their friends in the back. After a while, the organist went to his keyboard and began working his way through the prelude. Our organists were self-taught, and for that reason used the odd Klavarskribo notation invented by a Dutchman and favoured by self-taught Dutch immigrant organists. There was no piano in the sanctuary, pianos being unsuitable for serious hymn singing – maybe Canadian churches had them, but we didn't know about that.

Right before the service began, a line of men – first the deacons and then the elders of the church – would file up from the consistory room, reeking of cigar smoke, to take up their seats in a front side pew, at a 90-degree angle to the main body of the congregation, where I imagined they were placed to keep an eye on things. The elders and deacons were followed a minute or two later by the elder of service, who escorted the minister to the raised pulpit. The two men would shake hands, both before and after the service. The handshake was a sign the elders were the pastor's supervising body and that they supported the minister in what he preached that morning. I can remember only one occasion on which the elder of service pointedly refused the parting shake – the guest preacher had been a little iffy with a sermon based on the Song of Songs. It seemed he thought that the reference to the lover's breasts/pomegranates was not merely a metaphor for the relationship of God to his people, and that maybe we could learn something from that.

In short, church was a serious place. Every week the service had a ritualized confession of sin in which the minister read an appropriate Bible passage that pointed out the inevitable presence of sin in our lives and our need of God's grace, followed by a hymn of contrition, and then a brief announcement of God's forgiveness, a point that we didn't dwell on too long. One day our minister, forgetting who was in the congregation, changed things up and asked the rhetorical question, "Who among us has not sinned this week?" The father of my good friend Tony had the belief, in contrast to most of the history of Christendom and in defiance of his own behaviour, that once you believed in God, you no longer sinned. So he stood up, the full length of his lanky body, and in front of the entire seated congregation, boomed, "I did not!" And stalked out, right under the pulpit and out the front door.

We also had formal ways for dealing with sin. When I was five or six years old a young woman in our church had given birth out of wedlock and had to submit to discipline (a kind of formal and public judgment of disapproval) in front of the congregation. The nuances of this theater escaped me at the time, but I remember thinking it strange that the young woman agreed to be singled out for this public humiliation, and that the father was not present (not a member of our church, he was an outsider, probably a Canadian) – this last bit of wonder due not to an anti-patriarchal instinct on my part, but because babies always had both a mother and a father. That's just the way things were.

The central and longest part of the service was the sermon. The minister preached two each Sunday: one for the two morning services, and one for the afternoon, which would be based on the Heidelberg Catechism. As the minister began with the usual "Dear people of God," the congregation audibly settled into the sermon, with some shuffling in the pews and the sound of candy wrappers crinkling as peppermints were passed around, and the smell of peppermint would rise and mix with that of perfume and cologne. Other than the peppermints – sometimes two, if the sermon dragged – there was no allowance for the children in the congregation, who did their best. In later years some liberal parents would let their children draw or doodle during the sermon; mine did not. Each sermon was usually part of a series. When I was around twelve, a doleful series on Noah dragged on, it felt like for months, although I did perk up near the end when the minister tried to find something useful to say about Noah's embarrassed sons, looking away as they covered up their father's drunken nakedness.

And then, the hymns. The organist would meander through a bit of a prelude, return to the opening, and hold his "gathering note," a lengthy single chord designed to get everyone on board. It was full-throated, almost aggressive singing, the congregation not quite yelling at God, but powerful nonetheless. All Dutch congregations sang lustily, in working-class Dutch accents, with the "r"s slightly rolled, produced by a virtuosic interaction between a trilled tongue and pressure on the back of the throat; with immigrant mouths and lips incapable of pronouncing the English "th" without it thickening and coming out as a "d" or sharpening to a "t;" a "w" which could not escape sounding as a "v"; and finally the short "u" – the lips slightly puckered, and the vowel pushed up and forward in one's mouth. This was English learned on one's own, on the fly, far removed from the smooth British-inflected accents of today's Dutch people, accents which to my ears reek of serious education. That sound is now lost to the past but imprinted on my mind, and for all my different distances from that community and its ways of being, if I could hear that singing again, the sensory weight of it, as disproportionate and bodily in its effects as Proust's madeleine, would make everything else vanish, overwhelming me with emotion for my past.

Hymns were less a time of praise than of anxiety for me, of watching my father to see if he was going to be able to hold it together for this ritual, at least, maybe, this time. If I were sitting next to him we would hold the heavy blue hymnal together. Scanning ahead through the verses, I sometimes spotted a verbal prompt that indicated this was going to be a tough one, a hymn about suffering or death, say; at other times I had no idea what prompted my father's disintegration. Often, as the congregation launched itself into the second verse, I would feel the hymnal begin to shake, and, without looking at my father, I knew what was happening, and would grip the hymnal more tightly, fiercely but ineffectively trying to mask the shaking. Sometimes he would stumble through, dropping in and out of the singing, but doggedly making it to the end; other times he would give up and just stare straight ahead, his watery blue eyes looking into an imagined distance of space or time, as the people around us sang the stanza that on this particular day had defeated him:

> Though Satan should buffet, though trials should come,
> Let this blest assurance control,
> That Christ has regarded my helpless estate,
> and has shed his own blood for my soul.
> It is well, it is well with my soul.
>
> It is well with my soul;
> It is well, it is well with my soul.

Although church was a public place, I found some relief in believing that my father's stumbling through a hymn was private: no one could have heard his almost noiseless crying, and probably no one saw the tears and shaking, everybody having their heads buried in their own hymnals. We were alone.

He must have felt me clamping down on the hymnal extra tightly, and he probably understood that it was because of his shaking and crying, but did he understand what I, his youngest child, felt – protective, panicked, and embarrassed by him? That I, a modern son of Noah, wanted to help and comfort him, but that I equally didn't want anyone else around us to see, that I wanted to hide his nakedness? Did he know my anxiety, and, if so, what did he feel about that? Or was he completely ensconced in his own private world, the world around him, the world of his church and his son, having evaporated in the presence of his rising memory? When the hymn ended we sat down, looked straight ahead, and never acknowledged what had just happened. When I visited him at his church in the last years of his life, we would repeat the ritual, down to the last detail, except that I was no longer panicked or embarrassed. I just felt protective and, now, tired. This was never going to end; there would be no redemptive arc, no final years of peace and reconciliation.

*

My father's religious sense diverged from most in our circle, where his way of believing was an outlier. Dutch immigrants did not present their beliefs as something personal, but as something more rigorous than that, to be argued about and to set boundaries, boundaries less about including people than excluding them. Belief was about knowledge and propositions; it was theology.

But my father had faith. For him, faith was personal, emotionally intense, and something to be shared. This had always been the case with him, both in Amersfoort, with the men he met with for religious support; and after the War, when he joined a Salvation Army choir to sing on street corners, even though the church he belonged to had no truck with that unseemly brand of Christianity. And his faith was written on his body. During the long middle of my father's life, until his seventies when things began to careen out of control, his crying always erupted within a religious context – while singing hymns, reading scripture, or praying. So while his shaking and crying came out of a silence regarding its cause, and disappeared once again into that silence, his faith was the mechanism which occasioned and filtered things.

Belief propelled him, eventually, to tell his story, in an interview with a German pastor, in the book he wrote for his family, and then, much later, in answering some questions in a video interview for a local Christian high school. He did not tell it to bear witness to horror, to say that this really happened, that people are this cruel, and that we must remain vigilant, and never forget. On these occasions he told it to show God's ultimate power, that God had been with him through his suffering, and that his suffering could help others understand God's care. Amersfoort, on these occasions at least, could be a lesson. In his short book on the story of his life, just before he turns to narrate what happened at Amersfoort, my father stops to tell his children and grandchildren that, about Amersfoort, they "have a right to know and should know about the Lord's wonderful workings in this world and especially in my life." He breaks his silence to talk about God's providence, and for him God's providence went everywhere. Not just about his own history, but about other troubles in the world, even about climate change, he would always say, "The Lord is in control, Len." I heard this phrase, stated in exactly the same way, with the same finality of intonation, countless times over the years. No variation, no negotiating about that. Never even a dependent clause, something beginning with a "but" or an "although," which I would have welcomed. His phrase always closed off rather than opened up conversation, allowing his story no fuzzy edges. He never admitted that in the context of a Nazi punishment camp God's care could be an iffy proposition. He was not naïve about the sufferings of others, the millions who had died in the War, but he was so immersed in his own trauma and the presence of God in his own story that he never looked up – his own case was enough for him. Late in his life I got the courage to ask him, if God was in control, what about the others, those who never got out of Amersfoort, including members of his faith group. His answer was succinct, and either evasive or an acknowledgement of the limits of what one can know about God or about anything outside of one's own experience: "I cannot answer for the others; I can only answer for myself." That was as deep as I dared to probe. And, given what he had gone through, maybe that was enough – and, maybe my probing was a little patronizing, as if I, outside of and above the situation, looking down and evaluating, had a more distanced and therefore objective take on things. Perhaps my decades as a teacher and literary scholar took over. Perhaps the occasion did not call for conceptual rigour.

At first as a child and then as a young adult, I took his unwavering insistence as a sign of a steadfast faith, and his shaking and weeping as a tremulous sign of his hanging on to God, and a testament to me – if he could hang on to God after what he had endured, surely I, with my much lesser woes, could. And so, as a young adult I imagined him as some kind of heroic totem, out there on a bare promontory, face to the wind and driving rain, alone. My own struggles, about romances, job security, an uncertain medical prognosis, necessarily paled in comparison to near-starvation, being beaten, and watching people being shot and kicked to death. My issues were not worth bringing to the table, and certainly not an adequate source for religious doubt.

But his never admitting any doubts – that part of his faith gradually made me more and more uncomfortable. Not, at first, because I disbelieved it, but because it put him out of reach. His story was so out there, so beyond me, that a little religious doubt on his part would have been helpful, made him more approachable. But his unwavering insistence also began to trouble me in a different way, and by my mid-forties (my reassessment arriving a little later than it might have, although being immersed in a situation can make one obtuse about its possible alternate meanings) I began to have an additional, complicating take on it, sparked by that uneasy relationship between what he said about his faith and the marks of Amersfoort on his body and mind. If he, unencumbered by dependent clauses, really believed God was in total control, why all the crying? As I watched him, I began to see his non-negotiable assertion of God's care as a desperate staving off of something, and that "something" was not reducible to doubt about God's care. This shift in my perception of him did not make his struggles less authentic, less a demonstration of steadfast faith, but something more complicated. My father's unwavering assertion of God's care wasn't just a manifestation of his trust in a higher being; it was also something in addition to his faith. "The Lord is in control" wasn't just a proposition whose truth value could be tested; it wasn't central to him just for its content, but for what it *did*. From my vantage point it looked a lot like a way to clamp down on Amersfoort's horror. The phrase did something through its lack of nuance, its missing dependent clauses, its closing off the wildness of his story, its lack of doubt. In the face of horrific experiences, and as an attempt to give those experiences meaning, faith that gives no space for doubt looks much like a performative exercise of will, doing the same work as repression. This is not to disparage my father's very real, visceral faith. Every belief has its pragmatic side, and my father's religious beliefs were no exception. I don't think I need to choose between faith and repression in understanding my father: one thing being true doesn't have to make the other less so. For my father, his religious insistence was both real faith and an inadequate attempt at repressing the horrors of Amersfoort. And so, maybe my father's religious tenacity – exemplified by how his "God is in control" closed things off – and my mother's flatness when she took the Bible from his hands were mirror images of each other.

Weakness

I HAD AN AMBIVALENT relationship with my next-door neighbour Tom, a boy a year older and stronger than I, someone who had an undertone of aggression in everything he did and said. Although it wouldn't be accurate to say we were friends, I did like sneaking to his home some mornings and eating Honeycomb, a sweetened cereal that was one of the many Canadian foods my mother didn't believe in. His father was a distanced man who I wasn't exactly afraid of but was shy around, perhaps due to his stash of astonishing pornographic black-and-white snapshots hidden in his garage that Tom and I found and gaped at one day. I had seen porn before, in magazines stashed in an abandoned trailer in a field near my house, but this impromptu porn, black and white, on a home camera, featuring ordinary-looking people, in groups, doing astonishing things, somehow made it less staged, more unbridled, more real. Just across the fence, Tom's house, where the world was a little wilder, where one could eat sugar cereals and see porn, was a place where I always felt a little off balance.

I remember one incident clearly. About ten years old at the time, Tom and Rick (another friend from across the alley) were in Tom's backyard talking, while I mainly listened. They were talking about strength, and the comparative strength of their fathers and other men they knew. Their desultory argument over whose dad was the strongest morphed into one over whose dad could beat the shit out of whose dad if they wanted to. Rick had a plausible case. His father was a produce manager at the local Safeway and had to carry heavy boxes of fruit and vegetables. Tom countered with a robust claim for his father, and appeared to carry the day, but then Rick brought up his uncle, who lived with him. His uncle had a job bending steel pipes. And so, it was agreed: Rick's uncle could probably beat up almost anyone, and Rick basked in reflected glory. I didn't have a lot to bring to this contest. My claims were not that compelling, and I did not pursue them – my electrician dad worked with wire, which was both pliable and not very heavy, and he seemed more approachable than dangerous, certainly more approachable than Rick's uncle, who rarely spoke, was blind in one eye, and did not attend church. So I didn't add my voice to the competition. But I wasn't much invested in the argument anyway. It was not because in this discussion I was embarrassed by my father, or that I thought his crying implied that he was physically weak. To me, he just seemed outside of this economy of weakness and strength altogether.

*

Did my father get a pass because of Amersfoort? I don't know if that was the case back then (when I knew almost nothing of his War, but routinely saw its effects), but as I became older and Amersfoort's details began to surface, I started to think, long and heavy, about his crying and instability. It was hard to know what to make of it – was it a sign of a robust struggle, or was it the cry of a defeated man who for some reason could not find another response to his trauma, but repeated the same gestures over and over? During his crying episodes was he successfully warding off something, or had he succumbed? Outside of our immediate family some others were not so uncertain, particularly with larger cultural standards of masculine behaviour within easy reach, behaviours of stoicism and bravado, behaviours they thought my father could or should put on. But that's not who he was. In his last decades our family would hear occasional whispering by the residents of his rest home that, although he was a lovely man, so kind and gentle, he was weak, unable to deal with the past and finally move on. His reaction seemed a little disproportionate, didn't it? After all, the War had ended seventy-five years ago.

Maybe one should just walk away from this kind of inquiry. Who, from the outside, or even from a different place on the inside, could possibly judge another person's attempts to manage a life after having passed through one of the great horrors of the twentieth century? It seems disrespectful even to consider the question. But he was my father, and that changes things. His unreachable moments of physical and emotional stress wouldn't let me set the question aside, particularly as his symptoms became increasingly noticeable and harder to control. His counsellor let us know that my father's response to Amersfoort was on the extreme end of people with similar trauma. And pressing down on this professional assessment was my own unease, what to do with my own occasional impatience at him, my intermittent embarrassment, and my sense that he needed protection.

This is what I know: from an early age I instinctively understood my father could not be leaned on, despite his own wishes to be that kind of father. Amersfoort had turned some things around. In church, singing hymns, he was the child and I was the father, or he was a child and I was a confused orphan, muddling along. There were things I didn't or couldn't tell him, but not for the usual childhood and adolescent reasons. Not that I thought he was out of touch, or that he would be angry, but that he wouldn't be able to handle it. In early adolescence I suddenly started to run wild, two or three years in which my parents worried and tried out the usual disciplinary actions, to little effect. They could not reach me. And then one night, thinking through my day and its events, I had a sudden horrific thought, over-dramatized in retrospect, but viscerally convincing in the moment, believable to a receptive, troubled adolescent in a dark bedroom: given how I was behaving, it must be that I no longer believed in God. My equation between behaviour and belief was inevitable, given the legalistic community I had grown up in. But it was terrifying in its repercussions. My eyes opened wide and I stared up at the dark ceiling, my heart pounding, an existential loneliness pressing into my thirteen-year-old body. I was lost, the world had become an empty, windowless room; there was nothing above me to reach for. Sure, faith had never been that personal to me as a child; belief in God was just something I had assumed. But it had defined me, molded onto my mind and body through years of Christian school, hours and hours of Sunday worship, daily family devotions, weekly meetings of the Calvinist Cadet Corps. My entire life had been lived within the institutions of my immigrant religious community and bounded by my father's intense faith, and although that community wasn't really a cult, and people weren't actually shunned, once someone stepped outside of the community there were no occasions on which to see them anymore. They were gone. And so, the outside – of my community, and of my father's faith – was a world completely unknown to me, a boundless and empty space. But even though I wanted to, I couldn't call to my father to talk to him about my existential fear, to receive his wisdom and comfort. It wasn't that my father was like the other fathers in our community – distanced, unable to deal with anything personal. And I wasn't scared he would be angry or disappointed; he wasn't that kind of father, either. It was different: I thought he wouldn't be able to handle it, that my reaching out would precipitate an open-ended crisis for him, and so I was alone.

My father must have had his own ideas about his strength and weakness. I suspect he initially thought that keeping his silence and trying to force his crying into submission was a form of strength, keeping his pain to himself so that he could be a good father and husband. Successful – even partial – repression demands a kind of strength, although his wasn't workable in the long run. And from early on it was full of local failures that wore him and me down. Under my father's paradigm, which was the paradigm of his family and his culture, every time he cried, every time he left the room to lie down, every debilitating headache was a failure of strength. Only late in life did he come to accept the helpfulness of an acknowledged weeping, one that did not come out of nowhere and then disappear into it again. By then it was crying whose source we knew about, and about which he could and did talk. It was a modest improvement, helping to ease the local moment, but unable to slow down the march of years of damage, a march which broke out into a trot and then a run during the last decade of his life. Some things arrive too late.

My father did what he could with the tools he was given. Amersfoort debilitated him, making him unavailable to me at important times in my life, his own memories overriding my needs. But in most ways the concept of weakness is far removed from what he accomplished. He carried Amersfoort across the ocean, where he had to battle it on his own, in a strange country, where nobody wanted to hear it. He had to do it without his Dutch family, knowing that his family, through a multitude of signs, just wanted it to go away. He did it without knowing there were other ways of dealing with trauma. PTSD wasn't even a concept yet for him; it took him until his late seventies to think that maybe a second try at counselling could help in a way that a convulsive, aborted prayer couldn't. And when he began a new kind of counselling in his final decades, Eye Movement Desensitization and Reprocessing Therapy, he did not know what its endpoint would be – on a desperate gamble, he just jumped in. He was still getting therapy in his mid-nineties, still hanging in, still trying to rise to the occasion. And through all these years, with his terror always lurking around, cornering him, he remained gentle and kind, a quiet answer to the violence he had suffered, an answer I could hear to the very end, in his rest home apartment, as he whistled softly to himself while completing yet another puzzle that he could barely see.

But Here's the Thing

MY FATHER WAS also a happy man. Although his lifelong immersion in the War could feel as if he were adrift, by himself, on a grey and vast ocean with nothing on the horizon, his terrible moments and days were relieved by islands, sometimes whole continents, of contentment. He found or stumbled into moments of respite, and he savoured them. These were not ecstatic moments, but smaller times of contentment, when the world seemed hospitable. His smile, when he was contented with a good meal or immersing himself in a beautiful view, could be beatific. At ease for the moment, he would lean back, close his eyes, and sigh with pleasure. He was at peace puttering in the greenhouse he built, content playing his harmonica (a favourite tune was "The Happy Wanderer") or smoking his pipe. He had a substantial model train set, complete with a switching yard, town and station, and papier-mâché mountains and tunnels. He regularly took me fishing, and was perfectly content with modest success, three northern pike for the freezer. He enjoyed reading *Reader's Digest*, the *National Geographic*, and Popular Mechanics' *Home Handyman* (although he never took on any of the projects I wanted him to, like building a speedboat or private airplane). And he had a period of paint by numbers, whose seascapes we hung in our hallway. In short, he absorbed himself in all the clichés of white post-war North American fathers. But he loved them.

His most contented moments came on car trips and camping with the family. After hectic moments of packing, my father would sit on the trunk to force it to close, and off we went. Ten minutes later we were back, having forgotten some crucial item (on one occasion he had to drive back several hours to pick up the forgotten tent poles while we waited in the darkening campground, anxiously looking for signs of rain and bears). Our neighbours would place bets and watch for these ignominious returns. But eventually we left for good, and once on the highway we settled down. At some point my father would sigh contentedly, smile at my mother, and reach across and pat her on the knee. And sometime later she would quietly respond with "Wat ben wij toch rijk" (We are so rich). And then he would begin to whistle, or together they would sing a hymn or "The Happy Wanderer" in their beautiful and embarrassing Dutch accents. Unlike during his struggles at devotions or when helpless in the vise of a flashback, in his times of contentment my father forgot the War; these moments completely absorbed him. They were a gift, a modest exchange for his dark moments and days.

And he could laugh – full, open, head back, tears in his eyes. He laughed with others – that was the point. In our house at times we laughed so hard the neighbours could hear. My father would laugh hilariously when he would wipe out on a toboggan run or join in a water fight, and even found it hysterical when my sister Elisabeth, prone to manic outbursts, flung whipped cream at him. He threw it right back. He delighted in his children's inane antics, and he had some of his own. With my own children, he would pretend to be a billy goat hiding under a bridge, and run out at them, two furled umbrellas standing in for horns. I can see my toddler son, hands on his belly, doubling over with laughter, sometimes so hard he fell down.

Dirk Diepeveen, Untitled, *ca.* 1970

Of course, even in our dour immigrant Calvinist community a few other families laughed like this, too. And I have met others who replicate the odd edges of some of our laughter, our laughter in the face of misery: our laughter at hiking in torrential rain, or ineffectively pushing a car out of a snow drift, or being treated abominably by wait staff at a restaurant. It was our family instinct not to complain or to wallow in the misery, but to laugh it away. That particular laughter had an edge, pushing unpleasant things to the side, refusing to acknowledge them for what they were. People do this.

But in our family's most charged context – family devotions – laughter took a weird turn. It was almost always I who got things going at the end of a meal – a slight kick at one of my sisters under the table; or establishing eye contact with a sibling and then, poker-faced, slowly crossing my eyes; or (my favourite in its deviousness) just slightly jiggling the table – always a signal to people whose eyes were tightly closed, but whose arms were folded and rested on the table in prayer or attention, that someone was unsuccessfully suppressing a laugh, and thereby causing others to burst out laughing themselves. It wasn't just the joy of getting a laugh, a joy to which I am still inappropriately addicted. My attempts to get my sisters or father to laugh at the start of devotions, or even during prayer, had a polemical edge, a kind of self-assertion on my part, an assertion I only partially understood, an attempt to control where things would be going, short-circuiting my father's ritualistic dance/struggle with God and the War. I was a young boy, trapped, baffled, and anxious; what other tools did I have? And so, my strategy always succeeding, the table would shake – not from crying this time – and my father would laugh so hard that he needed to put his Bible down and sheepishly surrender. Another family ritual.

The ritual's disruptive impact was clear, but its meaning ambiguous. As was the family way, we did not probe that meaning very deeply, though we recognized what had happened as a pattern. Once there was no suppressing the laughter anymore, my frustrated mother would say in Dutch, "Daar gaan we weer" (here we go again), as everyone except her laughed. Curiously, her irritation did not boil over; unlike other occasions when I would be punished for bad behaviour, I was never sent away from the table in disgrace for having interrupted prayer and the word of God. Reprimands would be doled out, but not always, and then only mildly, and only by my mother. My father, perfectly capable of administering discipline on other occasions, had stepped back. A year after my father died, Nelly, my eldest sister, now in her seventies, recalled my misbehaviour, and in our first decent talk together about these moments of devotions-ending laughter she told me she had found it a relief when I began to knock things askew, that she would want it to happen – anything to stop yet another night of emotional tumult.

While in these moments I did try to disrupt my father's piety, I wasn't exactly working at cross-purposes to how his piety *worked* for him. And I think my father may have sensed what was going on; he knew what laughter could do. On one of the few occasions on which he spoke about his attempts to keep Amersfoort at bay, he referred to his own almost compulsive joking as a "big smokescreen," a way of hiding his inner torment from others. At times his and his children's manic laughter seemed to do similar work, holding things at bay, shoring things up. Repression in a goofy form, perhaps, but doing the same kind of work as my father's unwavering religious insistences. Maybe, probably. Anyway, you work with the tools you have at hand.

KAMP AMERSFOORT: ASSESSMENTS

Attempts at Rebalance

I LEFT HOME for college at eighteen, and after that returned only for a few years of summer work and after that visits of one or two weeks, as often as I could manage. The distances separating my father and me were far, my life became more complicated, and so for a few decades we saw each other at most twice a year. At first, my visits were to my childhood home, then to a condo in Abbotsford, British Columbia, and finally a rest home in Surrey, closer to Vancouver. While they were still able to travel my parents would visit Susan and me in graduate school in Illinois, and then later in Halifax with our children. On these later visits they were wonderful grandparents, engaged, fun, my mother with a touch of eccentricity that at times modulated into something more startling. On passing a nude beach on one of our oceanside hikes, she unaccountably turned to my horrified, straightlaced eight-year-old son, Benjamin, to tell him that, if she were just a bit younger, she would strip and join them, right now. It looked like fun. "I think I'll go walk with Grandpa now," he replied.

Particularly as time wore on, my visits to my father had a set of recurrent rituals, the first of which occurred in the initial moments of our seeing each other. Once he reached his mid-sixties, the age I am now, our initial greeting modulated, and I found myself looking at him for evidence of the ravages of time. He had always been a young-looking and handsome man (directly after the War his nickname was Ike, after the then-attractive American general), but in my twenties he began to age quickly and visibly, his posture increasingly stooped, and his hands and body shaking more and more, so that by his mid-seventies he had trouble eating soup or using a fork and knife to cut his food, and his writing gradually became less and less legible, and eventually impossible to decipher.

The crying at devotions didn't drain me anymore, the way it used to. I was older, no longer searching for a protection he couldn't give. I didn't live there anymore. As our visits drew to a close, I had the usual regrets of children visiting aging parents – that there were things we should have talked about, finally gotten to the root of, forgiven each other for. But I never initiated these talks with my father. I didn't want to be the cause of (and, to be truthful, have to deal with) a new bout of crying and the difficulties it would raise for him, and for me. No doubt I had internalized behaviours from childhood family devotions. When we left he would always thank me for coming, we would hug and I would kiss him, but he wouldn't look me in the eye, and he turned away, beginning to weep. We silently acknowledged that we were not together anymore but had built or continued our own lives separately.

*

At one point during those middle and later years, about forty years after he left Amersfoort, when I was twenty-six and he was fifty-seven, my father, fuelled by increasing flashbacks and nightmares, finally began to talk, deliberately, with a purpose. He had heard of a program in the Netherlands that gave counselling to camp survivors, but he was too apprehensive to go. Yet he needed something. He made an appointment at a local Christian counselling centre. The choice of a Christian counsellor was deliberate, my father believing his trauma to be an affliction totally entangled with his faith, and that it could be solved only through strengthening that faith. He drove up, parked his car, walked to the door – and turned to the side. He walked back and forth for a few minutes, trying to convince himself he didn't need counselling, that there was nothing wrong with him. And then he went inside. The first visit began disastrously: the counsellor, perhaps proud of his linguistic skills, or perhaps practicing without a licence, started things off by speaking to him in German. My father, initially paralyzed by a language he thought he had left behind and wanting to bolt from the room, accepted the counsellor's resultant apology and decided to stick with him, believing that he needed to separate his trauma with Nazis from his feelings about German people in general. (As it was for all Dutch immigrants, for my father the sudden eruption of the German language in his new world context, a context supposedly torn free from the War, was not just startling, it was a physical assault, impersonal yet brutal.)

As a further part of his new approach to Amersfoort, in the fall of 1985 he agreed to speak to a church about his War experiences. It was not to his Dutch immigrant congregation (he never spoke to it about the War), but one of German immigrants, in a different denomination in a different town. So he and my mother drove the hundred kilometres to an unfamiliar Baptist church on a Sunday afternoon.

His speaking is recorded on a cassette tape which my father gave to me about ten years afterwards. I listened to it for the first time on March 16, 2023, the day before my father's ninety-fifth birthday. It had lain in my desk drawer for decades, through most of my thirty-two years of teaching and the first years of my retirement. I had not forgotten about it, but on the occasions when I saw it lying in the drawer among non-working pens, obsolete computer cables, and old receipts, something always shut down in me and I would close the drawer and occupy myself with other things. But on that day in 2023, after spending the morning and the day before doing more urgent and evasive things, I dug out and dusted off an old tape recorder from the basement, inserted the tape, pressed the button, and began, finally, to listen.

My father's evening in this strange church, the evening before Remembrance Day, begins with the pastor announcing that the service will include a talk from Dirk Diepeveen, a concentration camp survivor, after which the congregation sings a hymn. The pastor has chosen "Onward, Christian Soldiers." And then my father begins to speak, his first public articulation of what he had gone through forty years earlier. The old cassette tape has deteriorated over the years, and his speech has taken on a warbly sound that defamiliarizes his voice, just a bit. He speaks slowly, with long pauses, and begins by saying that just a few months ago this visit would have been impossible. This evening is momentous, and not just that he is talking about Amersfoort, but that he is talking about it to a German pastor and a German congregation. Although he points out that the Dutch and Polish guards were often more cruel than the Germans, Germans, by the fact of their nationality, were a problem. He moves back and forth, first saying, with a stuttering apology to the people present, that at the time he hated Germans, but then later convinced himself he did not, until later still he had to admit that yes he did hate, but has now realized the folly of hating an entire people. That circuitous admission behind him, he begins his account of Amersfoort. He does not provide either a linear narrative of his time or many "gory details" about what happened at Amersfoort, stating that he does not want to dwell on the horrors, but on God's steady presence. He is in a church, not recounting facts but giving his testimony, and the genre calls for a closed narrative, a narrative not of wonder or ambiguity or doubt, but of certainty. He recalls the fellowship and strength given by his small group of fellow believers, and says he lost "some precious people," including members of his faith group of four, one of whom jumped off the train on the way to Gronau only to be shot and killed.

He notes that over the years he has been silent about Amersfoort, a strategy which he was taught right from the moment of his freedom, and against his initial wishes. He blames no one – "nobody knew about PTSD until Vietnam" – but now has begun to regret his silence. He tells or confesses to his congregation of strangers something about his response, something that he had never told me: "I never talked to my children about it. I had trained myself. I realize that was unfair." He is aware of the force of repression, of the nightmares enabled by his enforced silence, including a repeating one in which he is trapped behind barbed wire, unable to get out, creating an anxiety which he describes as having a hold that is "something fierce." "Nightmares became part of my life," he says, "and then you have to go to work." He accepted Amersfoort's black cloud as his daily companion, and his life had a rhythm, back and forth, between the exhausting force of his trauma and daily routine. That pattern lasted over forty years, until he could no longer go on unassisted, solely relying on repression to steady his wobbly life. He tells his audience he could never forget. As was his way throughout his life, at this point he gamely tries out a joke: "When I met my wife I forgot everything. Even after thirty-five years, when I look at her I still forget everything." He was joking, and he meant it. But he is also aware that his humour was a tool of repression, and calls his being a joker a "big smokescreen." Then, a long silence, followed with, "I couldn't share with my wife – I just couldn't. Having been silent for so long, I couldn't open up. I just couldn't."

And then the tape stops, midsentence. When I hurriedly flip it over, my father has vanished. The recording is incomplete; someone forgot to turn the tape over when the first side filled up. Whatever was going to follow, is gone.

My father's tentative beginning that evening loosened something. Five years later he started writing an account of his life, including the War. Self-published, with a cover illustration by a grandchild, it isn't long. It is a book with an agenda; in his foreword my father states that his purpose in writing is to "show to the reader that God is in control of our lives and it is utter foolishness to think that things are just happening in the world." The book begins with a "voor de oorlog" section that mainly includes whimsical stories of his youth, burnished by the glow of happy memories, untouched by the War or its memory, and one story so clichéd it has to be true:

> I had a brand new pair of klompen and decided to go sailing. A nail through the sole was a mast, you made a little sail, tied it to the mast and with a string let it sail onto the canals. In the excitement I forgot about the string and in my mind I still see the little boat sailing away into the sunset. Going home on one klomp was no pleasure, and neither was there any pleasure when I arrived home.

Then, as he did with my mother at home in their stories from before the War, he draws a line in his mind. There is no seamless transition to the next period in his life. Instead, he ends the story of the happy pre-War period of his life with, "Well, before long, Germany invaded Holland, resulting in the start of the 2nd World War for us." Then, on a separate page, in a paragraph all by itself, my father has a meta moment. Knowing he finally and without evasion needs to turn to the missing "oorlog," he addresses his children and grandchildren:

> I realize that it would have been perhaps better to have verbally told you about all those war years, but the scars are, at times, still very painful for me. I have thought about it, but it would be impossible. Maybe after you have read this book, there may come times when it will be possible.

Reading that passage for the second time in my life (like my father, I have had my own evasions about the War), almost forty years after they were written, I understood the words, and registered the intended force of the "you," but I just stared at them blankly, not finding myself able to rise or respond to the emotion he had when writing it – a moment of my own inadequacy, and perhaps lack of forgiveness, that discomfits me. But whatever their effect on me, for my father those sentences took courage. Writing his book not only required emotional bravery, but as with his post-traumatic life in Canada, he had no models for how to set about writing a biography – he hadn't been a big reader, other than newspapers and magazines, and he certainly didn't read things about the War. After that apology/apologia to his family, my father's book turns to the War and becomes explicitly polemical, like his speech to the German congregation an articulation and defense of God's leading in his life. In Amersfoort, he writes, "the devil sure was busy making us all feel totally forsaken and lonely, but God was more powerful and surrounded us with His love and care."

His book marks the start of, or enabled, a change in my father. In short and widely separated bursts, under internal duress, he occasionally began to refer to his experiences in conversation, which is not the same as talking about them. He never sat me down for a long talk to finally explain to me, face to face, the story of what had happened to him – only his book did that. Mediation makes some things possible, if only partially.

And somewhere during this time he tried something else to come to terms with Amersfoort, an act of either forgiveness or confrontation. After being freed from Amersfoort, he had returned with his family to Loosduinen, the signs of his incarceration publicly visible, his body still emaciated, his head still shaved. And there, in public, he met the person who had forged his identity papers so clumsily a few months earlier. My father had not revealed this person's name to his interrogators, and so had probably saved him from a fate similar to that which he had endured. But it was not a happy reunion, the forger taking the opportunity to publicly humiliate and bully my father for his appearance. This, for my father during his middle years in Canada, was the hardest thing to forgive. But sometime during the 1980s, on a trip to Toronto, he decided to address at least this one thing that might yet be resolved or fixed. The inept forger had also left the War behind, settling in Toronto, where perhaps he told his children about his heroism during the War, his dangerous work helping people resist the Nazis – which it was. Or perhaps he was silent. My father found his address. It was not hard to do; Loosduinen was a small town, and the network of Dutch emigres was efficient. Even those from the tiniest villages in the Netherlands could manage inevitably to locate their neighbours from the past, should they wish to. So, address confirmed, my father went to seek him out, to talk, and perhaps to forgive. Something open-ended, probably, but something that would take the pressure off. He knocked on the door, someone answered, and yes, the forger was home. But he refused to come to the door, and my father, left standing alone outside a closed door, turned and went back to his hotel.

small town and the network of Dutch contacts was sufficient even those from the tiniest villages in the Netherlands could manage inevitably to locate their neighbours from the past should they wish to. So address confirmed, my father went to seek him out to talk and perhaps to forgive. Something open-ended, probably, but something that would ease the pressure of it. He knocked on the door, someone answered and yes, the farmer was home. But he refused to come to the door and my father left standing alone outside a closed door turned and went back to his hotel.

The Right Proportions

WHAT MY FATHER wanted from the forger is unclear to me. The trip to Toronto was his only active attempt to achieve some kind of encounter with someone who had wronged him during the War, whether an encounter of confrontation or of forgiveness, he never told me. What I do know is that it was not the kind of coming to terms that he had hoped for, but an unsettling non-encounter, leaving in place an historical imbalance that refused to right itself.

A clearer outcome, one of either recrimination or of forgiveness, would have given a more satisfying shape to my father's response to the War, but such satisfying encounters do not come easy or often. In a text I worked with several times in my teaching years, Primo Levi's memoir *The Periodic Table*, Levi, in his post-Auschwitz work as a chemist, finds himself corresponding with a German counterpart who has a familiar name and a way of incorrectly typing "naphtenate" as "naptenate"[7]—the same tic as Levi's Auschwitz supervisor, years earlier. In "a state of violent agitation," Levi decides to press, to see if this Müller is the same Müller who, as a Nazi, oversaw his work at Auschwitz (as he indeed turns out to be). His purpose in seeking out Müller is nuanced: "Not to take revenge; I am not the Count of Montecristo. Only to reestablish the right proportions, and to say, 'Well?'" And Müller wasn't the worst of Levi's tormentors, not having been outwardly cruel, and having shown Levi some small kindnesses – a pair of shoes, permission to shave. Müller's lack of a crisp outline creates a bit of a letdown, Müller not being "the perfect antagonist" that Levi was looking for. Levi's desire for a storybook confrontation bumps against reality: "as is known, perfection belongs to narrated events, not to those we live."[8] Instead, Müller, "neither infamous nor a hero," was "a typically grey specimen."[9] Reality does not conform to the abstractions we think most useful for our personal needs. Levi writes of his own untidy reality that "this story is not invented, and reality is always more complex than invention: less kempt, cruder, less rounded out. It rarely lies on one level."[10] After some writing back and forth, Müller calls Levi and proposes a meeting in Italy, a meeting Levi does not desire, but "taken aback" by the voice at the other end of the line, he agrees. The imperfect confrontation was to happen within a matter of weeks. And then, after the two reach this agreement: "Eight days later I received from Mrs. Müller the announcement of the unexpected death of Doktar Lothar Müller in his sixtieth year of life."[11]

My father also did not get his storybook scene. He did not get to look the inept forger in the eye and say "Well?" if that is what he intended. If there was to be some kind of resolution, it would have to be without one of the partners joining in. He would be on his own, then, working out and measuring what had been done to him. Establishing the right proportions with those who had wronged him, and deciding the terms by which he would do so, was complex. In the last year of his life, my father in a phone call abruptly changed the direction of our conversation, which had been about the likelihood of rain in the coming days, to tell me of something he had suddenly recalled, something that happened during his week in solitary confinement in Elburg, before he was transferred to Kamp Amersfoort. My father was aware that a pastor who knew his family from Loosduinen had been recently transferred to Elburg. He asked the police chief if he could speak with the pastor's son, a boy of his own age, with the hope that the boy would contact his parents and let them know what had happened. The chief, in an act of kindness, agreed. My father says of the visit only that "it did not go well." The young man never told my father's parents of the visit, so they had no idea what had happened to him. And then right after the War, on the streets of Loosduinen, on the occasions when the pastor's son saw my father approaching, he would turn his back and refuse to look at him. After telling me this story, my father briefly said, "But I forgive him." And then he let it go and spoke of other things.

His telling this story moved and puzzled me. The story was gripping – another act of betrayal, a double betrayal this time. But that phone call was the first time I heard of it, and it unmoored me – still more devastation from his unending War. But most remarkable was his "I forgive him" – a judgment presented almost as a chance comment, an aside. It was the first time my father had spoken to me of forgiveness. The question of forgiveness in relation to his War had often been on my mind, but what my father believed about forgiveness had always been a formless shape to me. His reticence on that topic was not a surprise during the decades of my childhood and young adulthood. Since our family didn't speak of Amersfoort we also didn't take a further step, to speak of what we should think about it, whether forgiveness had a place here. And, except in isolated moments near the very end, my father didn't bring up forgiveness to me during most of his last decades, either. In those years, when his memories seized his mind and his body the experience was too violent for analysis; he was reliving his suffering, not responding to or analyzing it. In these moments panic was his only response. Small wonder talk about forgiveness was inherently rare.

But given time, the question of forgiveness as a way of thinking about and perhaps establishing the right proportions was inevitable, for him and for me. Even if you don't speak of your trauma, at some time you reflect on it, and on your response. Forgiveness is something for a time of reflection, when the trauma is no longer in the present tense, but the past. Thinking and perhaps talking about forgiveness suggests something has been thought through, assessed. As it does in novels, the quietness of past tense allows things to be measured. Periodically throughout his life, perhaps even daily, my father must have had to think through or confront his response to those who had hurt him. He had been wronged by many people, on many different occasions, in different ways, and to varying degrees. At Amersfoort, most noticeably by Joseph Kotälla, Commandant Karl Peter Berg, and the guards. But also the long aftermath of the War, beginning with the forger, and then those with clumsy questions about his experience, the German-speaking counsellor, those who whispered that he should just get over it. Finally, those closest to him: his parents and siblings and their enforced silence, my mother with her lack of empathy and then exasperation at the end. And me, I think, when as an adult I didn't give him what he needed, to the degree he needed it. But his life tended to be more about pondering than making decisions, with the result that he was a hard man to read.

His measurement of those who had wronged him had difficulty stabilizing, if indeed it ever reached such a point. As Levi points out, such finality, such cleanness "belongs to narrated events, not to those we live." In particular, my father's assessment of Germans wavered over time. His testimony to that German congregation in the mid-1980s – when he refers to his unsettled and changing attitude, moving from hatred to not hating, and back and forth one more time – reveals the stresses and fractures in his ethical assessment of others, in which at times he seems to watch himself try to do something he doesn't quite believe in, as he works to convince himself that he didn't hate.

One might think that, given his intense faith, my father's version of coming to terms with people in his past would be a response to and overlap with biblical concepts of forgiveness. After all, scriptural thinking on forgiveness is right at hand for a person of serious faith, which he was. Forgiveness is required ("as the Lord has forgiven you, so you also must forgive"), practical for one's salvation ("forgive, and you will be forgiven"), and infinite ("Peter came up and said to him, 'Lord, how often shall my brother sin against me, and I forgive him? As many as seven times?' Jesus said to him, 'I do not say to you seven times, but seventy times seven'").[12] But, while I am certain that he reflected on the relation between what he was thinking of people who had wronged him and scripture, it is striking that, in the moments when he spoke to me of what had happened in his life, he didn't reach to scripture as a model for forgiving one's enemies, and point to moments in his own life when he did forgive others.

Profoundly religious as he was, when my father told his story, neither the spiritual necessity nor the virtue of forgiveness was the point. The purpose of his War story, and of his surviving his suffering and then living with it was not about himself, but about God's leading. He wasn't presenting himself as someone to be emulated – he was too self-effacing for that. His story, when he told versions of it to others, pointed away from him. It's one thing to use God as a model, it's another to use yourself. (In his speaking to the German congregation he began by stating "I am not a hero.") In his book, written for his children and grandchildren, again, the point was God's presence – the book does not mention forgiveness. Forgiveness was not something he taught to others; it was not on a par with "God is in control, Len."

And when very late in life he on a few occasions mentioned forgiveness to me, he never presented the standard biblical injunctions as the reason for forgiving someone. He turned to something quite different: forgiveness was not so much a virtue as something that was necessary. Not forgiving was destructive, a secondary imprisonment. On one of my last visits, he spoke to me of a family friend who had also lived through Amersfoort, but could not let go of his hatred and ultimately, my father said, "drank himself to death." For my father this was a terrible direction: "The one that hates, he runs around with that load, day and night. But the one that is being hated may not even know that they are being hated, or if he knows he doesn't care. Actually, hate is suicide. I don't have hatred," he concluded, and then turned to speak to me of God's leading in his life.

Even if my father did not often directly refer to it, his grappling with forgiveness, even reconciliation of a kind, manifested itself in his life in a variety of ways. My father was not a vengeful man, and he was capable of great empathy, even toward his apparent enemies, an empathy that near the close of his life he revealed in the complexities of two incidents that occurred right at the end of his imprisonment. He had often referred to the bombing that had devastated Gronau, which, along with dysentery and the frozen fingers that prevented his leaping from the train, were the fortuitous triad of things that effectively ended his incarceration and prevented his death. But only in his final years did he add further context to these final days, and his assessment of what he experienced. Upon leaving the train car and being marched to the school where he would suffer further degradation, he saw the people of Gronau screaming and running blindly through the ruined streets in the aftermath of the bombing. Rather than walking along blankly, or thinking that their terror was well-deserved, he told me he felt sorry for them, and saw them not as enemies, but as human beings. A few days later from that moment in Gronau, my father, on the train platform, trying to find his way home to Koekange, was assisted by his friend's father, an act which he saw as an uncomplicated act of kindness. Both this act and my father's judgment of it I had known for some time. But only near his end did my father reveal that his helper was an enthusiastic Nazi collaborator, whose instincts on what to do must have been a tussle between an allegiance to a dying cause and basic human kindness.

My father's reaction to Joseph Kotälla, Amersfoort's camp commander, was also complex, though in a more puzzling way. I heard, indirectly and some years afterwards, of a difference of opinion with his mother at the time when Kotälla was scheduled to be released from prison. Kotälla had initially been condemned to death in 1948, but his sentence was reduced one year later to life imprisonment. In 1972, two years after my father carried the flag for Bevrijdingsdag and I asked a shameful question, the Dutch minister of justice proposed to release Kotälla, a decision which resulted in huge protests across the Netherlands, with the minister requiring special protection, even needing to go into hiding for a time.

A special inquiry was called, and the Dutch Parliament, in the face of enormous public pressure, decided not to release him. Kotälla remained in prison and died there in 1979.[13] The scandal inevitably but briefly broke the family silence. My grandmother, never deviating from a life of stern inflexibility, and labouring under who knows what psychological freight both from her son's imprisonment and her own legislated refusal to address it, ended her decades-long silence and stated she was adamantly against the release, wanting Kotälla to remain in jail until his death. My father thought differently, that there was nothing to be gained from a longer imprisonment, and that Amersfoort was all so long ago.

I'm not sure what to make of his reaction, whether this was a moment of forgiveness, or whether his response came out of other aspects of my father's character, aspects congruent with forgiveness, or with motivations for it, or simply characteristics that could mimic it: his exhaustion, or his gentleness, or his passivity. My father often referred to his exhaustion from dealing with the War, and as a result his wish to settle Kotälla into an unreachable past ("it was all so long ago") may have come out of his fatigue, a desire to leave it all alone. Perhaps he was too tired to imagine what could be accomplished by insisting his tormentor remain in prison – to use a phrase of my mother's, when she didn't want to talk about the past: "What is the use?" Or maybe his exhaustion had pushed him so much that all he had left to protect himself was passivity, a trait which increased as he grew older. His gentleness, too, had overtones of this passivity, as did his self-effacement. Perhaps these characteristics made forgiveness easier, or perhaps they stymied his ability to forgive. Moreover, all of these, like his insistence that God was in control, could both be what they were and also be a tool of repression. Letting Kotälla go meant he didn't have to deal with him anymore. And I could, I suppose, sweep all of this off the table: his wish to release Kotälla could be a sign of strength – not a timid man's surrender of his virility, a capitulation to forces that had flattened him, but an act of transcendence, a decision to stand apart, outside of all this noise. From my position on the outside, unable to look in, the perfectly clean and understandable motivation, like Levi's desired perfect villain, may exist, but in my attempts to understand my father I can't reach it. What I am left with are guesses and wonder, but that too means something. There was privacy around his forgiveness.

Over the long span of his life, my father also tried to come to terms with the people in his life who through signals both clear and subtle did not want to hear about Amersfoort or the difficulties of living in its wake. His attitude became more visible and less generous over time, with a complexity whose depth was unclear, perhaps even to him. Was he disappointed, even angry about their not wanting to hear his testimony about God's grace, or was it about their being uninterested in what had happened and the damage that had occurred, and uninterested in hearing how he tried to work through things, or perhaps that they were uninterested in *him*?

He felt the disappointment most sharply in his family, a disappointment that began as soon as he arrived in Koekange in 1945, when the familial unwillingness to talk about Amersfoort was presented, and perhaps understood, not as cowardice or evasion, but as pragmatic, as a belief that silence was the path to healing for my father – and besides, there was food to be put on the table, a job to be found. My father reported, as his letter from his father suggests in its practical intent on finding my father a job, that the attitude was

"Work hard, forget about the past," an attitude he eventually bought into for decades, succumbing perhaps to family inertia. That inertia required some thinking through for him. Speaking to that German congregation in the mid-1980s, in what sounds like the beginning stages of someone trying to work something painful out, and something I find hard to digest, he states that at first he wondered why his parents wouldn't speak with him about Amersfoort, but after some time he changed his view, and now forty years later, in what I heard as a moment of stunning but mistaken empathy, he believes his parents didn't want to hear because "as a parent, you know, can you really listen to some very bad experiences your child went through? You know, it is very hard." After a pause, in a steady voice, he concludes, "So, I don't blame them for that."

That was then. Thirty years or more after he made that statement exonerating his parents, in the last decade of his life, he revealed for the first time the anecdote about his mother seeing him approach Koekange, going into the house and closing the door, leaving him alone outside. It was not that he was just relating what had factually happened – the moment, like all moments he shared from that difficult winter, had become emblematic to him. Near the end of his life, with his parents and all his siblings deceased, he had an increasingly bitter take on the familial silence. In a mix of sorrow and anger at parents who could not rise to the occasion (or perhaps did not understand the nature of the occasion), he repeatedly expressed his frustration at their closing their ears to him, and at his siblings for not responding to the book he had written. But they were now all out of reach, should he have wished to clear things up. My father did not die with everything cleaned up, never came close to what the paradigms of closure suggest, with their narrative neatness premised on forgiveness, or at least a coming to terms.

As for our own nuclear family in Canada, two things stand out, neither of them clear or settled. Regarding my mother, his reaction varied between silence and a very occasional frustration. He never spoke of what he felt when she would take the Bible out of his hands, when her reaction to his manifestations of trauma seemed flat rather than sympathetic – whether he saw her actions as an approved form of silence (best simply not to acknowledge what was going on), or as one of resignation and criticism, in this case her actions revealing him, to his children, as inadequate, him sitting at the table with his head bowed while she brusquely moved things along, in a different direction, without him. Only very late in his life would he voice his frustration to me at what had become increasingly apparent in her response to his War: her controlling behaviour, and her inability to be empathetic.

And at one point in his talking to me his thinking about forgiveness in general crystallized, and this time he did frame it in terms of his faith. During a phone call in his last year of life my father, instead of speaking slowly, with the usual great pauses between his sentences, became increasingly agitated, cutting me off, wanting to tell me something, urgently. Under an internal pressure I could neither see nor understand, he let me know that in response to a sermon he had been thinking about forgiveness, and without naming names or specifying situations, he told me, "I forgave long ago. You forgive but you don't forget, because if you forget then you forget what God had done for you to carry you through that time." In the pressure of the moment, he presented that as a final coming to terms, a confident assessment. Were things now finally settled, a conclusion of sorts, a summation of his struggle with the War and his years of living with it? Perhaps, but neither was it the last word. That word, as always, belonged to the War. Several days later, he had a panic attack in the dining hall, and it took three caregivers to bring him to his room, give him Ativan and calm him, and then leave him to sleep. After they left, Amersfoort rose up again, and he spent an hour by himself, screaming and shaking, calling for God. Forgiveness, whatever it meant for him, may have helped my father, but it didn't fix things.

*

Forgiveness moved in two directions for my father. He attempted on several occasions to address the failures in his own silences and evasions, in particular acknowledging his shortcomings for not speaking to his own children about his trauma, that his silence, as he said to that German congregation, was "unfair" to them. I have wondered whether, minutes later in his talk, he connected that admission to his exculpation of his own parents' apparent inability to listen to their "suffering child." And as for me, I did not hear his apology until I dusted off the tape recording decades later, a lateness on my part which points to my own pattern of culpable silences and evasions. A few years after my father's admission that Sunday in a strange church, however, I did encounter a similar statement: in his book, where this time I was one of the addressees, though a continent away at the time. There it wasn't so much an act of contrition as an awareness of his shortcomings, and a reasonable explanation of its cause, that it "would have been perhaps better" to speak to his children about Amersfoort, but his pain over what had happened had made that too difficult.

And then nothing, for another thirty years, until, on one of my late visits, as we sat together in his apartment quietly talking, he told me that there were things he could have done better, that he didn't give me the life he would have liked to give, and he asked my forgiveness. He didn't say which "things" he could have done better; it was all very general, and he indicated that he didn't want to wade into the details. Both of us wanted to acknowledge the past, but we also didn't want the open-endedness and lack of control that specificity might unleash. So I did not press, and we did not make this the kind of reconciliation talk shows are made on. We kept things safer, more general. I think I did kind of rise to the occasion, telling him that, in the aftermath of Amersfoort we all failed – how could we not? – but that we all did the best we could with the difficulty we were given, and that was enough. I was okay; don't worry. In retrospect, this doesn't sound as generous as it might have been; I could have offered something stronger, more affirming, and, perhaps, something more confident, confident that I knew where the balance of culpability and grace lay. Once again there was an imbalance that has been there my whole life, an imbalance I still don't comfortably live with. It is impossible to know the right proportions when one thinks about forgiving someone who, though they may have wronged you in the ways that all people who love each other yet miss the mark do, is also someone who has suffered deep trauma, trauma out of which misjudgments and failures inevitably spring. There are no right proportions. Amersfoort took all normal equations off the table. In any event, ours was a kind of reconciliation, one based on the implicit rather than the explicit, on inferences that we made but did not share with each other. Murky, perhaps, but for all that a moving experience, both in how it addressed and how it evaded things, once again.

After watching him for more than sixty years, I don't feel like I have much to forgive my father for. But my coming to terms with others in his life is more complicated. My mother? She did what she could with what she knew, and what her models were. It got us through, and if at the end she collapsed under the weight of so many years, on good days I find myself unable to judge. On good days, anyway. As for those who tormented him and those who ignored him, I'm unsettled. There is something untethered in me that I don't know what to do with. I can easily summon my anger at what happened, and how the War just would never leave him (or me) alone. I don't know how, or perhaps don't want to, let that go. But I'm okay with my father, and that is enough. What Levi wrote about his antagonist could also be written about forgiveness: "reality is always more complex than invention: less kempt, cruder, less rounded out."

Memory, Discrepancies, Documents

MY MOTHER'S FAMILY has its own war stories, but most are no more than anecdotes, such as the story of my other Oom Arie, a sailor who found himself trapped in Italy at the beginning of the War, and over a period of months somehow made his way home to his wife, my mother's sister, my Tante Lien – up Italy, over the Alps, across Vichy France, through occupied France and Belgium, and finally into the Netherlands. Arriving at his home in Scheveningen, he knocked on the door. Tante Lien, when she saw him at the door, not having known whether he was alive or not, or what had happened to him, did not immediately let him inside but first made him strip, cleaned him with kerosene, and then shaved him all over to get rid of the lice. Then he was welcome to enter. As I heard my mother tell me this, it was clear that there was nothing odd about any of it, nor anything to dwell on. It was a typical anecdote from my mother about her family: all her stories were short, matter-of-fact, disconnected, and left me gobsmacked at the end.

The story she told the most, and with the most relish, was one about her father, my Opa Spaans, a man I never knew. The little I gathered about him as a person was that in the first decades of the twentieth century he was a fisherman from Scheveningen, a small fishing community on the North Sea. At some point he moved to another village nearby,

Loosduinen, where he sold fish, in the early years from a dog cart. My mother told me that he looked very old for his age and died before his time from that untreated and infected boil on his neck. Did my mother remember much more than that about her father, more than what she told me, he having died when she was eight years old? I doubt it. When I recently turned for more details about Opa Spaans to my extended family, my mother's remaining nieces and nephews, children of her much-older siblings, I got no help. The son of my Oom Arie said their father never told them anything about his father, other than an anecdote about once getting in trouble over spilling a precious cup of milk. And from Tante Lien's daughter all I got was that when things became difficult the family clammed up. It wasn't just my father's family, then, for whom silence was a way of life. With just these meagre details to go on, my opa wasn't really a person to me, he and his dog cart unable to rise above being a familial historical curiosity. And it wasn't just the paucity of information; even should more details have been available, 1932 was a long way away to reach back for a connection.

I have one photograph of him. It's a formal photograph, done in a studio with good lighting. The portrait was an occasion. He is wearing a full black suit. It doesn't need to be a colour photograph; from his demeanor I know the suit is black. My opa stares into the camera from the deep past. His face is full frontal, his mouth set and unsmiling – a holdover, perhaps, from earlier times when one had to stay motionless to avoid blurring the image – but I read it as the sign of a serious man not used to smiling. He is balding (I inherited that), with a slightly furrowed brow and an intense, resolute gaze. This is a photograph of a man in his forties whose life has not been easy.

Opa Leendert Spaans, mid-1920s

My mother's story about Opa Spaans is odd in that it's not a story about something she personally remembered happening, it having occurred seven years before she was born. It was an anecdote, really, about an event in my opa's life, which is not the same as a story telling me about *him*, about what he was like. My mother relished telling this story for its conceptual quirkiness, but it also has a lot to say about how stories in her (and then my) family were transmitted, modified, remembered, and partially forgotten. The story goes like this: my mother's father was a fisherman on the North Sea. One day when the boats returned to Scheveningen harbor, other fishermen reported that they had witnessed a boat sinking in the distance, a boat whose identification apparently matched that of my grandfather's. Since no fishermen from Scheveningen knew how to swim, and none used life jackets, he was presumed to have drowned. The pastor came by to tell my grandmother, there was a funeral, and my grandmother after great crying resigned herself, put on widow's clothing, and set out living a changed and more perilous life. And so it was, for a period of time. Then one day, presumably right after the war had ended, she saw her dead husband walking down the street toward her. He told everyone that his boat had strayed into restricted waters, and that he had been picked up by the British, and being from the neutral Netherlands but apparently suspicious or mistaken for a German, he was imprisoned for the rest of the war, and only now released to return home. My mother was born six years later, and, always with the same intonation and pacing, she ended her story with "so I was born of a widow, by her husband who had died years before." When she told it, it didn't sound creepy.

This is the only story of her life my mother wrote down and sent on to a few relatives. She crafted her story, particularly that final sentence. She usually didn't end her stories with this kind of summation; her stories just dropped. I was always particularly intrigued by that "so," which summed everything up, closed off wonder and other interpretations. A kind of crescendo, it points to her narrative and analytic powers. Her quip makes this story mean one thing, one thing only, and the thing it means is restricted, without nuance, and not that deep. Time to move on.

It remains, and can't move beyond, a family anecdote. Anecdotes remove the burrs from reality and polish it up. They summarize a way of life, a characteristic, a history, perhaps a person, standing in for a time or for a whole culture. And they have a point. They illustrate something; they don't stand alone. The anecdotalist works like a caricature artist: grab one characteristic, event, hang onto it, and sketch it so that it stands out in its isolation, perhaps even exaggerate it. A *family* anecdote has a particular purpose: it is one way to keep a person from getting lost to time. Family anecdotes give a synecdoche in place of the whole person, nothing rounded out or filled in, but it's better than nothing. Such compressing of a life is inevitable; time eventually boils down the life of a loved one to a characteristic smile, an enthusiasm for a particular food, a way of walking with hands clasped behind the back. And over decades even that gets wispier over time, till the person is gone, perhaps existing only genetically, in the shared arch of an eyebrow, or a tendency to Parkinson's. My mother's story was the one thing that wouldn't get lost to time, although it said nothing about who my opa was.

But those missing details in my mother's story bothered me. So several years ago I decided to work on tracking her story down, and if documentation revealed it to be true it would give my mother's anecdote some official validation, added weight to her telling, placing it in history. And if not... well, that would be curious. Over a few years I contacted historians on both sides of the Atlantic who did research on the First World War, one on the British history and the other on the Netherlands during that time. They concurred that it wasn't likely that my opa could have been a POW since the Netherlands was neutral during the war, but even had he been imprisoned, the Red Cross would have arranged for him to write his family. As a prisoner, he could not have just disappeared for a long time. But my British historian colleague pointed me in the appropriate direction in the British war archives, and so I did my due diligence there. As it turned out, the British kept very good records of their own imprisoned citizens but were not very energetic about those they had themselves imprisoned. My search turned out empty, although an archivist told me that there might have been records with the Red Cross – had their records not been sent to Switzerland, where they were destroyed by bombing at the beginning of the Second World War. The historian in the Netherlands, Samuël Kruizinga, knew of a few Dutchmen who were imprisoned by the British during the First World War for spying, but who would have been able to get in touch with family via the Red Cross or the Dutch consul. He concluded that while maybe I could just accept the family story as given, the evidence didn't support such generosity: "although I know of Dutch fishermen being killed in the North Sea, I have never heard of them being interned (as doing so would be contrary to international law)."[14] Apparently, my mother was aware of a lack of documentary evidence, and near the end of her life said she had been told that her father's imprisonment had been so cruel that the British after the war were ashamed and so worried about being found out that they burned all the records. In any event, whatever the plausibility of her explanation, no records of this possible event exist.

With all these holes, the family story began to sink under the weight of its missing details. Where was my opa during his time away? Possibly in prison in Britain, although it seemed more likely he just took off for a while, enjoying time away, perhaps even (to my mind, anyway, always hoping for something scandalous and tasty somewhere in our grim and grey family history) a fling in some other fishing port, a fling that perhaps gave me some new and friendly cousins in some brightly-coloured and sunny port in the south of France somewhere. But the only document I had that relates to this story, and then only tangentially – his photograph – does not suggest a man who could enjoy or precipitate a fling.

There was another way to go, and I decided to go there. Perhaps I was after truth, or perhaps I just really wanted to find me some grubby details. Kruizinga alerted me to the extensive Dutch newspaper archive, all searchable from my comfortable study a continent away. I entered two search terms for the years 1914–18: Scheveningen and Spaans, and sat down to rummage through 633 newspaper articles. The Scheveningse Spaans were a large family, with repeating names. According to convention, the first son is given the name of the paternal grandpa; the second son gets the maternal grandpa. (I am the second son; I would have been Leendert, but my immigrant parents, wanting to be Canadian, and sensing possible playground bullying for having a funny immigrant name, settled for Leonard. The name's success was mixed.) So I started looking for male names from within my mother's nuclear family: her father Leendert, and her brothers Arie and Piet. There were a lot of men with those names in Scheveningen. I held my breath when I came across a Spaans among the names of those lost in a sinking early in the war – a false lead, and on I went. I learned of a possible Spaans relative who was a partially successful comic vaudeville actor, going by the stage name Spaanio; of a legal tussle among several Spaans men; of the death of fourteen-year-old Arie Spaans in an accident; of a Spaans who was a renowned deadbeat; and of a Spaans who got in a brawl with his skipper (also named Spaans) after refusing to work and instead going below decks to find dry socks, and of the skepticism surrounding his testimony in court, he being a famously terrible employee. And then, about five hundred articles into my search I found it, in a lengthy article in the *Haagsche Courant* of 26 November 1917. It is an interview with my grandfather. The family story was wrong.[15]

Actually, it wasn't really an interview; there was no back and forth. The *Haagsche Courant* article was a transcription of a man uninterruptedly talking off the cuff, all in all a thousand words of my opa. The exhilaration of that moment of discovery is hard to overstate. There he was, suddenly a real person! The outline of the story he tells is simple. On the night of Monday the twelfth of November, four Dutch fishing boats (loggers) were sunk by German torpedoes thirty-five miles off the coast of the Netherlands. Before they were sunk, the crews (forty-eight men) were taken on board the warships for a day, as the ships made for the port of Wilhelmshaven, from which the fishermen were transported to Bremen where they waited for permission to return to the Netherlands. The fishermen made it home to Scheveningen on the following Wednesday evening. All in all, an adventure of nine days.

The events of the real story don't make for an improvement over the one I had lived with all my life. With its climax happening right at the beginning and the rest being a denouement, the new story had no punchline. It had no narrative arc, either in terms of plot or character development. The actual nine days of time are less than the implied years of the original, more suitable for a two-minute news story than the sweep of *Doctor Zhivago*. There is no delicious unknown time, a time which made for a better story, a story with more wonder. And so was he a bit of a disappointment, maybe, this new opa? I had kind of wanted a scallywag in my family, and his escapade would have been at the right distance. While a story of a secret second family is not what a person might want to hear about their own father, it seems fine for a grandpa, or someone further distant. I would have welcomed a second family; it would have opened up richness in character, along with new mysteries.

But finding this story, anticlimactic as the narrative was, was invigorating. Like a ghost, my opa, a real person and not just a figure in an anecdote, appeared out of the silence of the past and of his family. To be sure, I lost a good narrative, and the legendary, possibly ne'er-do-well opa disappeared, to be replaced by this more ordinary opa. But this opa was not just a narrative element, he was a person with things to say, and his own way of saying them. While I initially wondered why, of the forty-eight men who had been captured by the Germans, the *Haagsche Courant* chose to interview him, an ordinary sailor, and not someone else, such as the skipper, it became clear that my opa had a sense for and memory of details. A good source, he gives a detailed account of the sinking: that the Germans planted two, then three bombs on his ship; that they confiscated a couple of compasses and a clock, as well as a barometer and a lug clamp, and that in sinking the ships the Germans sent twenty tons of perfectly good herring to the bottom of the North Sea.

As I read my opa's account, my attention slipped to the side of the narrative, listening for his voice. I had been looking for a story, but found myself looking for *him*, for the person telling the story. With a new kind of information to find I read differently. It was clear, right away, that I wouldn't find who he was at his core, inside: unlike today's interviews, the interview gives nothing about his emotions – his fears during the sinking and his time on board the ship, or his anxiety about returning home, or the jubilation upon his return to his family. The closest approach to deep feeling occurs at the conclusion of the piece when he obliquely refers to the scene at home:

> We arrived in The Hague at 9:30 in the evening, and by 10 we were back in Scheveningen. Our family had received no word of us the entire time we were aboard the warship and in Germany, and until last Tuesday believed that we had drowned. The curtains were drawn here for three whole days.

"The curtains were drawn here for three whole days": not something direct, but a metonymy, I guess, for the sorrow that must have been felt at forty-eight men having drowned.

I strained but couldn't hear if in this major newspaper my opa spoke in Scheveningen vernacular, since Scheveningen vernacular of the 1940s was the origin and emotional basis of the Dutch I knew. Scheveningen Dutch was just Dutch to me; I had no standard Dutch with which to measure it by. A lot of the article was in the kind of talky Dutch I knew, the Dutch of my mother – a casual tone of voice of a confident narrator, quick to make value judgments that were all understood to be common sense. Opa occasionally referred to his reaction to or understanding of an event as "natural," or prefaced a sentence with an "of course," and at times would drop into a colloquial phrase – while in Germany, the fishermen "hadden geen cent op zak" (didn't have a penny in their pockets).

I was unsure what his words revealed about him, whether I was recognizing, really hearing, his distinctive voice in this verbatim article. My Dutch, passable in conversation but unaware of its infelicities or reliance on post-war slang, had trouble with the nuances of the language, and nuance is what makes a voice. Was I reaching when I thought I heard not just him, but an echo of my mother's voice at such moments, in phrases she also used, or was this just ordinary colloquial Dutch?

But I thought I did recognize something in the details that he chose to talk about, something distinctive that echoed my mother's characteristics as well. In the space of a thousand words he mentions food thirteen times, giving more attention to it than to the apparently accidental shooting of one of the fishermen by a German soldier. And he was judgmental. Although occasionally he found the food to be adequate, he more often wasn't impressed. Speaking acerbically enough that the reporter thought to put the word in scare quotes, he reported that on one morning "we were given 'coffee' again." German coffee did not impress him – at another point he referred to it as "so-called" coffee. And his captors didn't know how to prepare food. They gave him a "strange" roll which gave off a "sour smell"; the cabbage soup had unpeeled potatoes in it; there was an unpleasant spiced soup, which the fishermen traded for cigars and cigarettes. Worst of all for a Scheveninger, Germans did not know how to prepare fish; he reports that his lunch menu one day included "ongeschilde aardappelen met' kabeljauw (zonder vet)" – unpeeled potatoes with cod (without fat). The parentheses indicate a negative assessment that the *Haagsche Courant* needed to point to, my opa having made a parenthetical value judgment, perhaps pointing to it with an added twitch of his eyebrow or a baffled hand gesture. (My mother's family believed in fat – my Tante Lien once vehemently said to me, "It makes me furious when people speak against fat." Without fat, she believed, one's kidneys would shrivel.)

It is the food, and Opa's way of speaking about food, that reveals him to me, that fills me with a flood of recognition: for something familial, certainly, and perhaps for a person. I am not completely certain that I really found him, that instead I am like my mother with her failing eyesight, scrutinizing a photograph that she really can't see well, and seizing on an accidental detail in the background as a sign of something. In any case this is now my family anecdote, an anecdote partly about my opa and the family resemblances. Given the story's lack of a decent narrative arc, it has become more substantially an anecdote of my overturning a family story, of my finding him, buried in a newspaper of 1917. Not as cool as discovering the family quirks and wine of my cousins in the south of France would have been, but you take what you are given.

And then there was one more turn to the story. Almost a year after my father died I flew out to Surrey again to see my mother. I had been warned. After her most recent, third, bout of COVID she had not rallied as before. Her body was as strong as ever, but her mind, in the period of two days, had slipped into serious dementia. I became aware on this visit that my mother had retreated into her own kind of silence, that she was falling away from me. A talker her whole life, she now spliced unrelated sentences together, confusing things even further with her use of untethered pronouns that pointed in several possible directions at once. When I would ask who "he" referred to as she spoke, she would look startled and reply, "the person we are talking about." With a kind of muscle memory of what conversation sounded like, for two hours at a time she would unspool the ghosts of what had been her favourite topics, partial narratives spliced on to other narratives, and then onto worlds that her misfiring neurons created out of nothing, worlds where the King of the Moon was late for dinner. But still there were moments when she connected. I wanted one of those moments so I could relay her father's real story, a new story that I had uncovered just two weeks before, a story that overwrote/erased an old one, sure, but that also brought her father to life. I had my qualms. What would happen, would it displace the only story she had so proudly written down, and if so, was that a good idea, would she like the trade-off, hearing her father's voice, or would the change be impossibly confusing to her, would she be unable to process it?

When I arrived the second morning of my visit she was upset. An intercom's incessant buzzing next to her bed had kept her awake, she said, for hours. After I found the switch to turn it off, she suggested I take a walk for a half hour, but said I could stay if I were quiet, sitting in her chair. So, for an hour on a sunny morning I sat watching while she slept, on her side, breathing heavily and irregularly, occasionally murmuring something indistinguishable. When she awoke she was reasonably aware, so I told her about what I had discovered, and that her father had been captured by the Germans, not the British. But here he was, in his own words, to tell what had happened. I wanted to get the intonation and the pacing right, so I had practised reading the story in Dutch a bit, trying to recreate what I imagined were his pacing and enunciation, the pitch and roll of his voice, his Scheveningse imprint (reading "with expression," as my fourth-grade teacher would say).

I read it in my Dutch, which my cousins unkindly have likened to that of a drunk farmer. I'm not sure if through the filter of her hazy memory and my awkward pronunciation she heard her father's voice, but she smiled at the many comments about food, particularly his disgust at cod being prepared without fat (she grimaced at that), and she clearly liked the story. After I was done she did not address the radically different timelines in the two stories, but she speculated briefly about why she thought in her version of the story it was the English who had captured him – maybe because of a childhood book she had that her father (perhaps my father, her husband, right before their emigration?) used to learn English. Then her attention to the story became wispier and wispier, and soon she was off in several different directions at once. Three days later, at a moment nestled within her rambling, it was clear she was back to her original story, and that was the one she would carry with her to her end. It was the better story.

*

The porous family transmission of my grandfather's adventure resembles how and what I came to know of my father's experiences. Like all stories from the War and the experience of its long aftermath, my father's history has little gaps, small discrepancies, few documents, and substantial mystery. I have included in this book only one incident I know to be false – my apparent memory of my mother shouting at my brother to take my father away to be hospitalized, an incident more semiotically useful than true. But other anecdotes that circulated in our family, never to be resolved, are more an occasion for wondering – not just for probing their veracity, an activity which has become increasingly difficult over the years, but for thinking about their function, whether they fill in a gap, or whether they fill a need. I vaguely recall my mother (in the only time I recall her speaking of what had happened to my father) telling me a story of someone who was viciously beaten, or lined up with others and shot, for stealing a potato. Later, I understood it as a group of ten people, perhaps my father included, who were lined up, and three of them randomly shot. For most of my adult life I believed it was a guard who had set him free, telling him that he could leave to get his frozen fingers taken care of at a local hospital but that he must "promise" to return. However, in the year before he died my father indicated that it was the Red Cross that secured his release. Did I make up the guard story, or did someone tell me this, or do the two versions not really conflict, did a sympathetic guard release my father to the Red Cross? Confirming these details was difficult because in many cases I had no idea of the origins of these suspect details. They are like ghost ships, insubstantial, having appeared on my horizon from nowhere.

When I would tell others of my father's War, piecing its details together under great emotional duress, I never thought of turning to his book to straighten out my own account of Amersfoort. (Later, as my father began to speak of what had happened, it became clear that the account of Amersfoort in his book was itself partial, selective.) I did not structure my account with how he had narrated his time at Amersfoort in his book, a book I was unable to hoist myself to read a second time until I began to work on this memoir. It was my unstable memory that guided me. Even in my teaching that's the way it went. At times I would tell my father's story to my first-year students, as a prelude to the sessions we would be spending on *The Assault*. Sitting in my office before class, I would fidget, changing the formatting and indentation of my lesson plan, then changing it back and adding boldface in appropriate places, and then finally and abruptly stuffing the printout into my briefcase and making the short walk across the street to the lecture hall. It was a large class, 360 students, all with their eighteen-year-old heads down when I entered, looking at their phones. As the class began I would ask them to put their phones away, and on this day there was something in my voice that prompted almost all of them do so. As I began to speak I could not see many of the student faces past the third row, and with those students I did not make eye contact. I looked over them, into the distance at the back of the hall. And I would tell my father's story, a story that included a man standing in a line, awaiting and then surviving his execution, of being released by a sympathetic guard, of running away from shots being fired, wearing prison clothes with a large red target on his back. And this time, to this story of mine, my students did keep their phones put away and pay attention – one TA, years later, on hearing of the death of my father, told me he could have heard a pin drop as I spoke. I always told my father's story calmly but with urgency, realizing it wasn't pedagogically necessary, but young people needed to know, know what the consequences of cruelty could be, that these things really happen in this world, and that we need to pay attention. And then, my father's story concluded, we opened our books and turned to *The Assault* and had what passed for a normal class. I did not want to talk to my TAs afterwards, as I usually did, to ask how it went, what things I might need to clarify next time. Head down, eyes averted, I briskly headed out and off campus for coffee.

But as I told it to my students over the last few years of my career I began to wonder whether this or that particular event really happened. The prison clothes, for instance, clothes that would have made him instantly recognizable as he ran away from the train and made his way home. As I began work on this memoir I contacted researchers at the memorial in Amersfoort and discovered this detail to be fabricated, probably by me, without being conscious of having done so. But exchanges like this, from sources that could either corroborate or discredit, were rare. And as I thought about it, I began to notice a recurrent characteristic of these possibly apocryphal details. Some began to sound like exaggeration, perhaps even melodramatic embellishment – if one can ethically surmise such things in accounts of trauma. These kinds of details all made my father's story larger, more dramatic, more meaningful. As with my mother's story of her father, these details made for a better story. With these apocryphal anecdotes his story became less an account of blind survival, and more a hair-raising adventure with twists and turns. They made my father, if not a hero, at least the centre of an amazing story, and gave him, and me, more weight. They are my gory details, filling out a narrative, details that made the narrative pop, plot devices that, now I have discovered them to be false, a touch clichéd, a bit of theatrical overcharging, a Prussian dueling scar added to a villain out of *Sgt. Fury and his Howling Commandos*.

*

That is one direction things can go in filling out the silences of my father's War. But in the past few years I was provided with another approach to the silence, an approach not structured to provide astonishing new revelations, but one that immersed his time at Amersfoort in the mundane life of bureaucracy, of checking boxes, of forms and categories, and of accounting procedures. Late in 2022 I wrote to the memorial at Kamp Amersfoort, telling the staff there that I would like to donate a copy of my father's book upon his death. And I wondered if he had been the youngest political prisoner there – the fact that he had been just a boy at the time of his incarceration had increasingly troubled me as my own children went through their vulnerable adolescences. After a short delay, I received a reply. A staff member, Eddy van der Pluijm, gave the bare outline of what the experience of an Amersfoort prisoner would have been at the time, the precise dates of my father's official incarceration, and a few clarifications.

And he attached a gift. At the end of his email were scans of my father's Amersfoort documents, six pieces of his official record: his initial admission record, which included the place of his arrest, his home address, occupation, religion, and next of kin; his name in a ledger with other prisoners, indicating place of origin, date and place of birth, and date of incarceration; two financial records which balance, one individual, and the other a larger ledger that included other prisoners; a single document in German, this time with his name misspelled, indicating his admission date (January 13, 1945) and his final transfer date (February 5, 1945); and what looks like an individual transit record, to the concentration and labour camp Neuengamme. On each document the primary finding aid was his prisoner number. Before opening the documents I stared at the email for a while, thinking that this was it, this would finally do something. I would cry, sure, but this time it would be what people call a "good cry," and after that I would rise up healed, blow my nose, dab my tears, and walk tenderly smiling into a different world, a world not of anxiety and sadness, but of reconciliation and new directions.

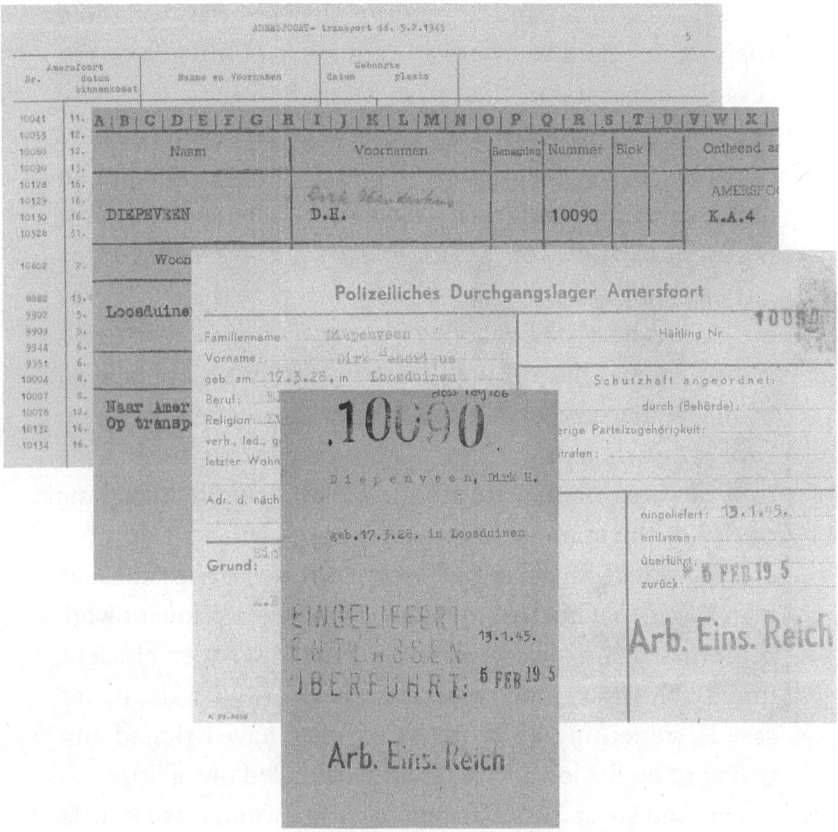

Kamp Amersfoort documents, 1945

It was pretty to think so. My plan collapsed as I stared at them, slowly scrolling back and forth, my breathing shallow yet again. And then, rather than being energized, I found myself back in a familiar emotional space: flat, weighted with sadness and weariness. I found myself unable to process the contents much at first, beyond noting what these documents looked like. They are printed on several colours of paper – beige, yellow, brown, green, and one pink, for an unknown bureaucratic reason. Some are printed on thin paper, no doubt to allow for duplicates or triplicates; some of my father's individual records seem to be on card stock. Some are ledgers neatly alphabetized; some, on heavier paper, are transit documents, related just to my father, and capable of being handled and exchanged. Two of the documents are in Dutch. And then the writing and printing itself, signals easier to read. Most immediate are the violence and bureaucratic clarity of the stamps, reserved for dates, prisoner number, and the classification of my father's offense against the German Reich, that he tried to escape Nazi conscription for work in Germany. Simple categories, pressed into paper: efficient, unerasable, final. One typist had problems with the uppercase H, something which, repeated, must have irritated him trying to do his job. (That raised H troubled me, a little too much. And so I pressed, trying to extract from it what little bit of knowledge it might release. Having been trained on a manual typewriter, I eventually realized that the raised H was due to the clerk having a weak little finger on his right hand, whose job it was to hold down the heavy shift key while the index finger of the same hand stretched and reached across for the H. The weak right pinky wasn't up to its job, resulting in a raised H.) Some documents had handwritten annotations: clarifications at times, but more often an indication that

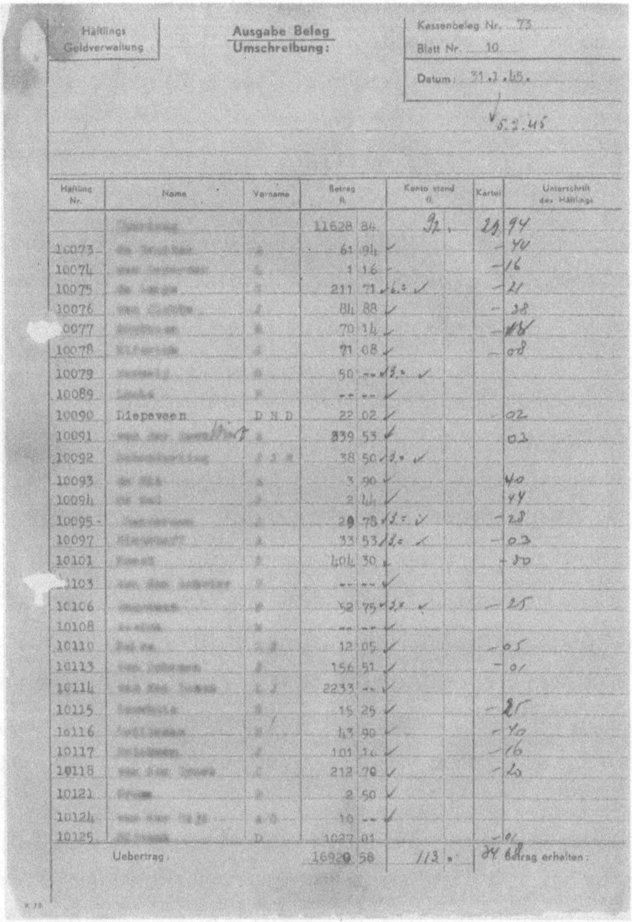

Häftlings Geldverwaltung

Ausgabe Belag
Umschreibung:

Kassenbeleg Nr. 73
Blatt Nr. 10
Datum: 31.1.45.
5.2.45

Häftling Nr.	Name	Vorname	Betrag fl.	Konto stand fl.	Kartei	Unterschrift des Häftlings
	[illegible]		11628 84	92.	21	94
10073	[illegible]	[illegible]	61 94			44
10074	[illegible]	[illegible]	1 16			16
10075	[illegible]	[illegible]	211 71	6.=		21
10076	[illegible]	[illegible]	84 88			38
10077	[illegible]	[illegible]	70 14			18
10078	[illegible]	[illegible]	71 08			08
10079	[illegible]	[illegible]	50 --	3.=		
10089	[illegible]	[illegible]	-- --			
10090	Diepeveen	D H D	22 02			02
10091	[illegible]	[illegible]	839 53			03
10092	[illegible]	[illegible]	38 50	3.=		
10093	[illegible]	[illegible]	3 90			40
10094	[illegible]	[illegible]	2 44			44
10095	[illegible]	[illegible]	29 78	3.=		28
10097	[illegible]	[illegible]	33 53	3.=		03
10101	[illegible]	[illegible]	404 30			80
10103	[illegible]	[illegible]	-- --			
10106	[illegible]	[illegible]	52 75	3.=		25
10108	[illegible]	[illegible]	-- --			
10110	[illegible]	[illegible]	12 05			05
10113	[illegible]	[illegible]	156 51			01
10114	[illegible]	[illegible]	2233 --			
10115	[illegible]	[illegible]	15 25			25
10116	[illegible]	[illegible]	43 90			40
10117	[illegible]	[illegible]	101 16			16
10118	[illegible]	[illegible]	212 70			20
10121	[illegible]	[illegible]	2 50			
10124	[illegible]	[illegible]	10 --			
10125	[illegible]	D	1027 01			01
	Uebertrag:		16920 58	113.=	34	68 Betrag erhalten:

K 73

Kamp Amersfoort Prisoner Financial Registration Card, January/February 1945 someone was checking documents to make sure everything tallied. Together, the documents exude self-assurance, silence, serenity. To my mind they have a confident personality, the pencil checkmarks on the financial documents smug in their efficient certainty. No violence here: simply a bureaucratic response to a minor offense.

The documents did what they were intended to do. Everything added up, sometimes twice – no accounting mistakes here, everything justified, reconciled. What they were supposed to do for me is less clear. They did nail things down in one way – not to show that Amersfoort really happened (of that I never had doubts), but I now felt more profoundly that my father's suffering was not just something private, shuttered within my family, but that it really was a part of *history*. It was a recorded part of big things. The documents also could do something more, I hoped; they could add specificity, with dates and places; they could show some of my own ideas about his story to be true and others not. With their actual dates, places, and official reasons for his incarceration, the documents extended the boundaries around my understanding of my father's trauma, moving it beyond his intermittently disbursed and anxiety-filled memories to the silent certainties and flatness of Nazi efficiency. The flatness did its own work; my knowing the life the documents encircled made their impassivity and silence more, rather than less, horrific. The documents created a contrapuntal effect within me, both of constriction, of a life and event bounded and encircled by something large and authoritative, the gravitas of numbers and classifications; and then within those confines my own father's story – particular, emotional, unbearably sad – fizzed and rattled around. The crisp record-keeping also had a function Amersfoort's clerical staff never could have imagined:

they were central to my father getting restitution, and to his marking it in a way that I love, with a big family party, and aimlessly circling around a lake in a paddle boat, with his children on shore, laughing and laughing.

The Amersfoort documents record basic details about my father: his birthdate (March 17, 1928) and place (Loosduinen), home address (53 Prins Hendrikstraat, Loosduinen), religious affiliation (Protestant), occupation (electrician), next of kin (his parents), marital status (single) and children (none). Along with these facts, which I already knew, were clarifications and things put into focus. The mixture of Dutch and German on the documents points to something often bypassed, of my father's fellow countrymen's eager participation in Nazi violence, something that corresponded with his own sense of things: he routinely pointed out that the Dutch Nazis were among the most cruel guards at Amersfoort. On the transport list of prisoners to be taken by train to Germany, the one – partial – ledger I have that gives the birthdates of prisoners, my father is the youngest person, by three years, with most being significantly older. (I later discovered, through documents at the Dutch National Archive, that there were only three younger than him on that transport.) His being so much younger than those around him may account for the extremity of his reaction, if accounting is something it needs. Two documents raise more questions than answers, showing the money he apparently had on entry, but didn't spend – twenty-two guilders and two cents – what in the world could that signify? I have been assured by van der Pluijm that my father would have had his money returned to him, along with his clothes, when he was transported to Germany. In another instance the documents fail, pointing to nothing, perhaps. One of his transit papers, created by the Red Cross at the time, indicates he was going to Neuengamme. He and his fellow prisoners on the transport to Germany believed this was their destination, and that they would die there. But in an email to me, van der Pluijm writes that:

> On February 5th 1945 a transport left for Gronau and not as the post war registration card mistakenly states to Neuengamme. Once the prisoners arrived at the Employment office (Arbeitsamt) Gronau they were divided to work at factories in the area or in this case the prisoners had to dig trenches.[16]

Camp documents reveal that the only trains from around that time that were scheduled to end at Neuengamme left on February 2 and March 15. (Van der Pluijm attributes the Red Cross error, on a card that was created after the end of the War, to the chaos at Amersfoort that winter and spring of 1945.) So, in the archive there is at least one unstable document, one that raises rather than answers questions.

The documents also raise the question of that week when the transport train did not arrive and he was returned to Amersfoort, a return which does not show up in any of the records. But the gap is pointed to on my father's two final financial records, detailing that his money was returned to him unspent, and that all was in order.

The typewritten underscoring in the first document indicates, a little primly to my mind, that this was a final exchange. Financially, at least, everything on that date was balanced. Nothing more to see here – we're done, close the books. Both documents are officially dated January 31, the date my father was marched through the wet streets of Amersfoort to a train that never arrived, and then marched back again. The January 31 train is the train that by its absence forced his return

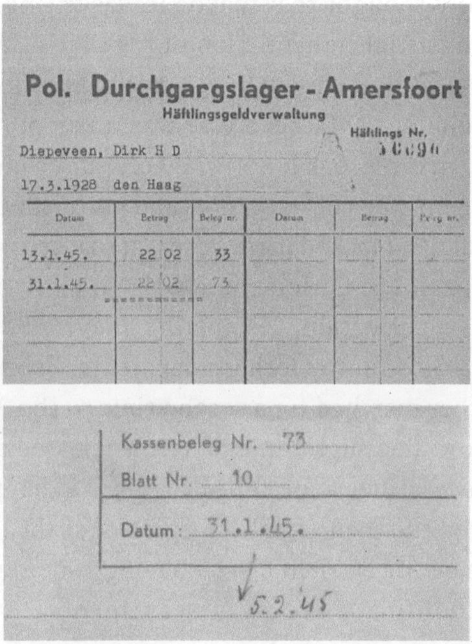

Pol. Durchgargslager - Amersfoort

Häftlingsgeldverwaltung

Häftlings Nr. [illegible]

Diepeveen, Dirk H D

17.3.1928 den Haag

Datum	Betrag	Beleg nr.	Datum	Betrag	[illegible]
13.1.45.	22 02	33			
31.1.45.	22 02	73			

Kassenbeleg Nr. 73

Blatt Nr. 10

Datum: 31.1.45.

5.2.45

Kamp Amersfoort Prisoner Financial Registration Cards,
January/February 1945

to Amersfoort for another week, resulting in his arrival in Gronau in the aftermath of a bombing, perhaps securing his freedom due to the chaos of the days following his arrival.

I initially thought that maybe it was fitting, given the uneasy and partial transmission of his time at Amersfoort and what have been my own apocryphal tendencies, that a crucial time in my father's War was unsupported by any document, that there is no official account of his return to Amersfoort, his week of starvation, and his freedom. But then, later, and calmer, I looked more closely at that second financial document, and the curious handwritten mark on its right side. It was a correction, designating a revised date for the money returned on my father's departure: February 5, the day my father marched for a second time to the Amersfoort train station. The slight emendation indicated a less than smooth process, that something irregular had happened here, an attempted and then a final departure – a silent acknowledgment, perhaps, of Nazi efficiency having gone slightly awry, but also a confirmation of my father's story.

Corroborating my father's account of his last week at Amersfoort may seem unimportant – a mild confusion over dates, what does it matter, balanced against the horrors of the War? What function might this confirmation serve? There is, for me, a small satisfaction in solving this one slight mystery, as someone who watched my father for decades. The clarified dates and what they stand for round out a narrative; the end of Amersfoort doesn't just fizzle out into something indeterminate, silent. That satisfaction of confirming things has always been a part of my life with my father, propelled by an at-times puzzling wish, coming more out of my own needs than an attempt to set the record straight, to affix my father's story into a larger history. My minor detective work makes me feel like I am *doing* something for him, that I am pointing, giving his suffering the attention and particularity it deserves. Careful attention can be a form of love. Brought to light, that week-long hole, previously outside of history, is important. It shows that my father's private memory fleshes out a public record, that he was right, that his memory has weight.

KAMP AMERSFOORT: LATE

Late in Life

MY FATHER RETIRED early, his shaking, headaches, blank motionless staring, nightmares, and flashbacks taking over too much of his work day, leaving him exhausted every evening. He had more than another thirty-five years left to deal with the War. Ten years after having left Edmonton to retire in British Columbia, my parents entered a retirement home, and ten years later, in their early eighties, to assisted living, and then eventually, for my mother, alone, to nursing. The usual trajectory. Over the course of this book, when I have used the phrase "late in life," I have been referring what became a new time for my father, pointing to several transitions, a shifting of gears, and an increase in speed. The phrase refers to their time in the retirement home, but also to the changing hold of Amersfoort on my father in those years, a time when he revealed new memories and increasingly spoke of that time, when his understanding of his trauma changed, when the War increasingly weighed on his body and mind, and when his relationship with my mother transformed and then collapsed.

As was true for his life in the first four decades after the War, my father's last years weren't all bad. For much of his final decades he was capable of his own brand of contentment and joy: playing the harmonica, taking walks, and participating in a writing club, where he wrote whimsical stories about life in the rest home and about good times both "voor" and "na de oorlog."

He did not write about the oorlog. His care for my mother was touched by his humour. When he went out on an errand while she was sleeping, he would leave her a cheery note and shaky drawing. Until he could no longer rise to the occasion, in the rest home my father took it upon himself to cheer people up. He did it with terrible jokes, which got worse with age and repetition, and at times provided a new kind of embarrassment for me. When asked whether he wanted a cup of coffee at dinner, he always said, "Just a half. The bottom half." (His prune juice, always, was his "power juice.") And he whistled, hymn tunes and "The Happy Wanderer," as he plodded with his cane or walker down the carpeted halls. The whistling was not just a sign of his contentment. He told me he thought it gave comfort to people whose lives were difficult. It did. The staff and other residents loved him. The abundant widows loved him, which irritated my mother – they liked him more than they liked her. During my visits they routinely came over as people were being seated for dinner, before the meatloaf was rolled out. They would lean over to talk to him, smiling nicely, and maybe touching his back, to assist with their balance, perhaps. He didn't flinch. As I was walking with him to the communal area to pick up the morning snacks on one of my visits, we approached a group of women sitting together on a couch. My father, hunched over, stopped, turned his head sideways and up to me so he could look me in the eye, and, taking one hand off his walker and grandly gesturing to the women, said to me in a voice loud enough for them to hear, "Len, these are the flowers of the rest home." In response came a wobbly treble voice, "But you are the root, Dick! You are the root!" The Root just smiled and walked on to pick up the coffee and bran muffins – if it is possible to strut while using a walker, my father did that. My mother called him a flirt, and she was right.

Cheery note, ca. 2018

Although they never completely left him, those moments became fewer; Amersfoort and its increasing toll on his mind and body dominated more and more. He would stand motionless for long periods of time in his slippers, loose sweater, and retailored pants (retailored to account for his osteoporosis, whose progression required that one trouser leg be hemmed three inches shorter than the other); wordlessly staring out the window, his pale blue eyes watery, looking into another world, and out of reach of whoever was nearby. At other times he would stand or sit with his arms wrapped around himself, not because he was cold, but to curb the worst of his shaking, which at times became uncontrollable and violent. His tremors at times accelerated to larger, almost convulsive motions, which he gamely referred to as his "Hitler shakes" – an attempt to deflect with humour, with a term both self-deprecating and defiant. Several times in the dining hall it took three staff members to restrain these tremors and take him back to his room. He needed special care when his trauma erupted, and at times people failed. Despite our explicit instructions not to do so, during a hospital stay nurses shook him awake from a nightmare, with the result that he needed medication to bring his hysteria under control. Although they didn't happen every night, these nightmares would leave him shaken, dazed, unable to rouse himself to a new day's modest demands.

Those disconcerting and frightening episodes were the culmination of a long, relentless trajectory. When my father was about seventy years old, his standard coping mechanisms, never having been very effective, became even less adequate for the task of getting him through his days. His standard responses of repression, prayer, and assertions of faith were not abandoned, but they were not enough anymore.

And so in 1997 he went back to counselling, but this time not to a Christian counsellor and faith-based therapy. No longer believing his trauma could be handled solely through religious approaches, he went to a counsellor who was practicing a new kind of therapy for clients suffering from trauma, something called Eye Movement Desensitization and Reprocessing Therapy. Having become available only in the past few years, EMDR asked patients to focus on a traumatizing image, and then with repetitive eye movements from side to side, or some other alternating physical sensation, allow the brain to desensitize the image and memory, and create space for more conventional counselling on how to deal with the eruptions of trauma symptoms in daily life.

As a result of his counselling, my father began deliberately and openly to refer to Amersfoort, slowly at first, and then with increasing speed. It wasn't easy – on the way home from sessions he would cry in the car, trying to speak to my mother and Elisabeth (who lived nearby, and took on the role of adult child as caregiver) of things that had happened at Amersfoort. His talking circled and circled around two traumatic events – the prisoners singing their way to execution, and the hollow eyes of the prisoner with dysentery, staring at him – and was always accompanied by crying. My father's Amersfoort became a circumscribed activity of speaking (and sometimes apologizing to his children for needing to do so) in short bursts that revealed not so much a story as an image, a sensation. But such references weren't as devastating to me as his crying when I was a child; no abyss opened up for him or me when he did cry, no sense of entrapment, no panicked fight or flight anymore. (Indeed, that reaction, that physical imprint of my father's story on my body, now only recurs when I, no longer a watcher but a speaker, tell his story to others.) The contract had changed for him as well: he needed us to listen, and wasn't as embarrassed anymore, as far as I could tell – although he did add his instinctive apology each time after I witnessed an eruption of his trauma, verbal or otherwise. The propulsion behind this change was uncertain to me: perhaps he found talk useful for taking the pressure off, or he wanted his family to know, or he needed us to know, or we were the only ones who could listen in the right way. But near the end he could not always control who his audience was, at one point having a flashback and anxiety attack in a dentist's chair and needing to tell the panicked dental assistant about its contents.

His EMDR encouraged him to talk about his past, and in an at-times disorienting temporal imbalance I learned more about the War and my father in his final decade than I had during my first fifty years. I learned details about the past, about Elburg and his time in Gronau, and especially about the silence after the War, his bitterness about it, and his mother closing the door when he was in sight of home – this one a story which he told to me not while looking down and away, but standing and looking me straight in the eye, wanting to make sure I understood what had happened, and by that, perhaps, its semiotic significance for him. That story was an unusual one. His details or anecdotes about the War were almost always disbursed in moments of panic, urgently, and ending in a sudden change of topic. And, very occasionally, a short talk, quiet, with clear parameters, as with the story about his mother. My father came alive to me in those final years; like many adult children, only near his end did I come to see my father as a full person, a person with complexities, regrets, anger, and moments of stunning grace and dignity – "God is in control" was only part of who he was.

It wasn't all about the War, this change in my relationship with him, and it wasn't always that my father had changed, but that I had, that I was looking at him from a different angle. Some of the alteration was the result of noticing his increasing physical vulnerability, of my rushing across the country and seeing him hospitalized with a respiratory illness, frail in his bed, looking both like an old man and a little boy as he slept, and his quiet smile as he awoke and recognized me, that I was with him again. There were small moments like this, such as my quietly entering his apartment and watching him contentedly enjoy a Mozart concerto, at times conducting it tentatively with one hand. Our talk with each other had changed as well. I began to deliberately tell him I loved him at the end of a visit or a phone call, and he started to say it back, perhaps initially over polite obligation, and then, over time, occasionally he would say it first. He would intermittently and briefly tell me of my mother's needs and difficulties, awkward though that often was. Nearing the end of his life, he began to speak retrospectively of himself and his career at work and in the church, of his pride in his work, he a modestly educated immigrant having eventually risen to become the Director of Program Development for the Alberta government's apprenticeship program. In that position he was particularly proud of his work with Indigenous youth, one afternoon shuffling across the carpet in his slippers to search in a drawer to show me a citation he had received from a tribe expressing appreciation for his work. He shyly smiled at me as he handed me the certificate to look at, a smile both proud and seeking approval.

And of course his new openness in talking about Amersfoort helped me to know him better, who he was, and why he was the way he was. But it's difficult to weigh how the change in his relationship to his memories of Amersfoort helped him – it provided some local alleviations, momentary easings of pressure, but along with this his deterioration, psychological and physical, gathered speed. The strain of Amersfoort became too much – in the predictable debilitating physical and psychological manifestations, and then in one way both unpredictable and devastating. His relationship with my mother deteriorated, slowly at first, and then with calamitous speed and effect until my parents could no longer live together. Both of them had changed; they both needed more, and their needs pulled in opposite directions. My father's symptoms and talking about Amersfoort increasingly dominated their home life, but my mother simultaneously became a different person, enhancing traits which had always been there, and had been central to her own dealing with Amersfoort for years. Each person's needs and characteristics made the other person's difficulties worse, and my father couldn't deal with that runaway positive feedback loop.

*

My mother was a talker, she always had been, but at some point her talking tipped over from eccentricity to something else. What it became still baffles me. In a social group, with people mildly chatting together, she would start in. Not addressing or perhaps not even being aware of the current drift of the conversation, she would begin to talk, and then completely stop interacting with those around her; but leaning forward, eyes closed, she would embark on a monologue – at times for fifteen minutes straight. No one could break in, interrupt, or change direction. Her talk was always about people, my mother having no interest in current events other than natural disasters. She would go over the marital history of a friend whose husband had died early, leaving the widow to raise four children alone, and which of that widow's many children had a good job, where those children were now living, how many children those children had; the terrible fires in northern British Columbia; the difficulty, for her, of my father's shaking; those grandchildren who were too fat or too skinny or depressed, don't you think; the niece in the Netherlands who hadn't called recently, and what must be wrong to cause her to lose contact like that. Those topics covered, she would circle back to pick them over some more. And everyone in the room would be trapped. The feeling of sitting in her overheated living room, trying to avoid eye contact with others while her talk washed over me was not exactly the feeling of being trapped at my childhood dinner table; it was less horrific but something more stultifying and maddening, leaving me wanting to jump up and scream in frustration to make it stop. If others eventually could find a way to abruptly insert themselves and change the direction of the conversation, she would lean back, become still, and look to the side, or up to a corner of the ceiling, waiting to break in again. A slight pause in the conversation, and off she would go, in a completely unrelated direction, sometimes prefaced with her routine transitional phrase, "But here again," a phrase gesturing to connection, but offering none. Her talk came as a great wave, unstoppable, and all we could do was wait for it to eventually stop. From the other side of Canada my nightly telephone calls to her became increasingly mystifying. After answering the phone and asking about our weather, she would tuck in and take off. I could not interrupt; she could not or would not hear me – one time I even tried repeatedly shouting into the phone to attract her attention, to no avail. Frustrated, in a mix of shame and defiance, I even set the phone down and attended to another task while she kept going for a half hour or so, counting on speakerphone to alert me when to grunt in sympathy or scandal. I couldn't figure out what she got from these calls, whose regularity she anticipated with relish. I could not understand why she was telling me these stories about the sister of a cousin of one of the staff at the home, who now had to contend with a broken leg after a car accident – and why she returned to that damn broken leg, every night, for a period of weeks. While telling me these things energized her, even at times took her out of her despondency, I don't know why it did. The content of her incessant talking didn't seem as important as the act itself; it seemed like she was scratching an itch.

At times her talk looked like a coping mechanism, a way to insert her own place and importance into a family dynamic that had been dominated for years by my father's War. But there seemed to be an added complication: her talking, overriding whatever was going on, redirecting things and seizing a new agenda, had the air of something familiar: a way of sidestepping, a form of silence, a mode of repression, a way to shut everything else out. While she was talking, my father and his Amersfoort could not intrude, and she could be her own person, for better or worse. This, of course, is speculation, but speculation is all I have. When she was talking I felt myself in the presence of something more private and baffling than my father's response to Amersfoort during family devotions.

The relentlessness of her talking was only one part of her transformation. She modulated away from an exuberant engagement with life to something dour. The change, like my father's downward slide, was inexorable and distressing to watch. Certainly, during my youth she had those awful moments when my father could not repress his trauma and she silently stepped in, putting the Bible and Amersfoort to the side. But my mother had often been happy during my youth. Once capable of an at-times anarchic joy, over her last couple of decades she stopped laughing and succumbed to the familial gloom that had taken her sisters and made their last years miserable for themselves and their families. This is not what my mother had wanted for herself. She had seen it in the family she had left behind, and she didn't like it. Never a cheery person, her oldest sister, my Tante Dien, became impossibly and unreachably gloomy and angry as she aged. In her room, on the tenth floor of a rest home that overlooked the beach at Scheveningen, she would rap on the window with her cane, angry and shouting at the nude sunbathers below. Taking matters into her own hands, she wrote the Dutch Queen about the disgrace that she was witnessing. I did not hear that the Queen replied. People could not bear to be in Tante Dien's company, a context in which everything was met with withering censure and gloom, and my mother, clucking disapprovingly about her sister, told me often, "If I ever get like her, Len, sla mij dood" – club me to death.

My mother's gloom wasn't manifested in abstract speculation about the nature of evil and suffering in the world; it was always specific, and its reach went everywhere. She spoke woefully about the horrible accidents that maimed or killed people she had heard about, and the state of Friday traffic in Vancouver; she repeatedly vented her displeasure at Elisabeth, her caregiver daughter who lived nearby, who spent too much time with her grandchildren and some days was not available to run errands for my mother, who needed bananas that very day, not tomorrow ("I have been put on the back burner," she regularly sighed with her exquisitely paced martyr's sigh);

she murmured against the carelessness of young parents, who were both too reckless with their children and gave them too much attention; she complained about the size of the portions in the dining hall (both too big and too small), the caregivers who ought to know better, and the people who didn't leave her alone but instead harassed her by wanting to know how she was doing after she had been sick.

Her talk would spiral, endlessly, around topics that consumed her. For three years or more, several times a week she would expound upon the problem of young women who wore fashionably distressed, ripped jeans. She wouldn't let it go, and we had to warn her grandchildren not to wear such jeans when visiting, or they would be cornered by someone who handled her anger at the trend with the ferocity of a ferret. Her monomania about these jeans was not what one might think, a residue of the War – a protest against the ridiculous cost, or the waste, or a dislike of the post-apocalyptic vibe such fashion emitted. Her objection was theological. In a phrase she obviously relished, she would say again and again, over a period of several years, "God is a god of wholeness, Len." Distressed jeans flouted the will of God, who wanted creation to be whole, pure. Somewhere in this amazing world there must be a cult that centres its rituals around the repudiation of such fashion. I hope so.

From a distance, with the mediation of print as one reads this, my mother's listed complaints are both dizzying and comic, their bathos a product of their stunning and diverse reach. And, for a reader, her complaints aren't relentless: one can put this book down, walk away, and leave it behind. And at times we children would step back and laugh at how awful my mother's gloom had been on a given day, the medals she would win if complaining were an Olympic event. But hearing it in person, or every night on the phone, the cadences predictable, rising and falling, never ending, is a different story, and for my father, living with such operatic gloom ground him down – her dour talk, unceasing and repetitive, filling every corner of my parents' small apartment, pressing into his trauma.

Although my mother gave no indication that she sensed the toll her gloom was taking on her children and husband, she did know we thought her despondency to be excessive. In return she asserted that she was simply being realistic. Her particular form of realism took their relationship further downward. For my mother, realism and practicality were the same side of the same coin, and they put their stamp on every aspect of how she lived with my father. She believed her realism and practicality gave her a superior sense of the dangers of the world, dangers unperceived by my father, whose lack of common sense, especially about how to deal with the War, routinely caused them unnecessary problems. Her job was to keep a lid on things, a task which became increasingly difficult in their later years, as my father's relationship to Amersfoort became increasingly fraught and visible. She did not respond well to these eruptions, but clamped tighter and tighter. As they slid downhill together her instinct was, as it always had been, to press down, not to bring things up. One day early on in my father's EMDR treatment, angry at the crying and talk that had been stirred up after a counselling session, she threw away his copy of a poem about appel at Amersfoort, a poem written by a fellow prisoner, that my father had saved for decades. She did not like talk about Amersfoort, believing that it went nowhere, that it had no use. Just get on with life. Less dramatically, she ran interference for him, steering him away from his heavy conversations with a relentlessly serious local pastor, or trying to get him to stop watching the news, whose stories of tragedy, she believed, only made his days – and, yes, *her* days – more difficult.

It became too much, for both of them. My mother eventually couldn't deal with his increased crying, or his embarrassing public tremor, or his vacant stares into the distance, a place she couldn't reach him. And she really couldn't handle his *talk* anymore, his new, counselling-sanctioned talk about the War which seemed to be the cause of all these other things. She wanted the War to be out of their lives, finally. Her protectiveness, keeping Kamp Amersfoort at bay, mutated into a hyper control, touching on all aspects of his life, from where he should sit and how he should use his pillow when he sat, to what he should wear on his feet (she confiscated and gave me his Birkenstocks because she said they made him trip over the little rugs they, in the manner of all old people, had scattered throughout their fully carpeted apartment), to insisting he not take his cane outside of the rest home (because he might lose it), to banning his doing jigsaw puzzles for hours a day, to eliminating sweets (a treat she didn't care for, anyway), to deciding on what they both would eat at a restaurant, so they could split a single portion. Their apartment became my mother's panopticon, and she did not blink.

Nothing of her strategy was negotiable, and my father, his passivity becoming increasingly visible, never pushed back. When by some accident during the day my mother's program was not followed, she became angry, pointing out that the negative results (his crying and nightmares) fell on her to deal with. In a phrase she repeatedly used after he did something she considered foolish (a walk too long, or watching the evening news that featured a story on refugees), she would angrily say, "Now I have to live with it." Her anger was also pointed at those – particularly her children – who thought they knew a better strategy for my father to handle his trauma, and who didn't know what it was like to live with him. His return to counselling, a further impediment to their life together, seemed to repudiate her life's work, which had been getting her children through to adulthood and my father to his final days without too much damage. No one was able to successfully push back against her strategy, and my father, with his lifetime of having enabled my mother's control, let her strictures increase until their life together became intolerable.

As many of the aged do, immersed in their end-of-life issues, somewhere along the way in her practicality my mother lost her empathy. Four years older than he, she became more demanding on him, waking him to ask for a glass of water in the middle of the night, or for him to fry her an egg at 4:30 in the morning, or to empty her commode (this despite his tremor). My father, his health increasingly fragile not only because of Amersfoort but also because his heart was giving out, started to check out. Increasingly deaf, until they were banned he turned to puzzles, for hours, his back to my mother, who suspected what was going on.

It is difficult to understand what drove her behaviour, behaviour that could seem at best inconsiderate or unsympathetic, and at times just mean. Part of it seems to be that she was terrified of being alone, that she was scared of losing him, her controlling behaviour propelled by panic as he deteriorated, the kind of panic that she described feeling at eight years old when her father died, and she was alone, in her home, in the dark. She needed him. For all her control of my father, she had always loved and respected him (she often referred to him as "the boss," which her children found hilarious), she had always leaned on him, for his sense of how the world worked, for his love, for his mere presence.

Her appalling moments, which I most often saw as an embodiment of her frustrated love or more simply as her desire for control, at times pointed in a different direction, to an assertion of her own needs. My mother had her own health problems, and one day she became lightheaded and slid against a wall and down to the floor, and insisted (contradicting her doctor's prognosis, something she routinely did, and with relish) that she had suffered a concussion – a diagnosis which she later reassessed as a stroke. Her accident dominated her talking for weeks. As we tired of it, and my father impatiently told her so, she countered, "I have my own trauma." And then, turning to my father, she said, "You get to talk about Amersfoort."

The clear-eyed cruelty of what my mother had said was obvious; what was less apparent was where it came from and what it signified. Its import, I believe, hinges on its disproportion, the mismatch suggesting her outburst erupted out of frustration. For years the attention in our family always centred on my father's trauma, and except for the occasional health emergency my mother's own problems always paled in significance. It is true, her fall must have been frightening for her. But even she knew it wasn't commensurate to what had happened to my father, and there was nothing she could do about that. Their life together was out of proportion, seventy-five years of it hinging on my father's five weeks in the winter of 1945. At times she must have wondered where was *she* in all this? Was she not an actor in her life, but merely a stage manager? And now near the end of her life, with her own infirmities and her approaching death – when was it her turn? A closed person, and not attuned to contemporary forms of psychological expression, my mother could never imagine saying, "But I have my own needs, too. What about me?" So while her statement about the equivalence of her and my father's suffering was clearly unbalanced, as was her controlling of his behaviour, theirs had been a life of imbalance. And in having to deal with that disparity, and the way it pushed her own issues to the background, she was not so different from me, whose life has also been one of uncertain space, its terms preset in another country, fifteen years before I was born. At times I understand her frustration, even her anger.

*

In the space of three months, with my parents' relationship groaning under the stress, two events made everything collapse, the years and patterns of their dealing with Amersfoort together becoming unmoored. The first was COVID. My parents' rest home was rigorous about keeping its residents physically safe, and so during COVID's periodic outbreaks residents were confined to their rooms, at one point for a few weeks, with meals dropped off at the door. There my parents were, together, twenty-four hours a day, with my mother's increasing controlling and erratic behaviour in full mode, unseen and unstoppable by anyone else, and my father increasingly emotionally and physically fragile at being locked in, a lack of freedom which increasingly triggered his anxiety and flashbacks. ("How wonderful," people would say to me, "that your parents, at such an advanced age, and in these difficult times, still have each other.")

Then, in their nineties, they both developed COVID. My father's case was mild, and he recovered after a week. My mother was a different story. Against medical advice, she had refused to be vaccinated, arguing that the flu shot always made her arm swell up. As her illness progressed, she insisted that we remove all medication and assistance – none of her pills, and no oxygen. She went downhill quickly; after a few days her blood oxygen dropped to seventy-five – significantly lower than the point at which oxygen deprivation begins to affect one's organs and brain function. We expected she was going to die. And then, on death's door, she bounced back, and when I saw her three days after her crisis, she was happy – unbridled happiness for the first time in years, a happiness which lasted three or four days, after which she settled back into her gloom with renewed, almost manic, vigour.

And now, with her unexpected recovery and her strictures on my father's behaviour reaching new levels of rigour, everything – their love and the seventy-two years of life they had made together, almost from scratch, unravelled. My father panicked. Knowing that my mother had wished to die, having seen the woman he had loved and lived with for over seventy years suffer, and seeing his ending days stretching before him again in lockstep with her, under great emotional duress he said to me, while my mother lay convalescing in the next room, "She should not be alive." We then both sat there silent for a while, acknowledging and feeling the reach of that phrase. He did not look up at me when he said it.

While I was growing up, and until this time, my father had been the most patient of men with my mother's eccentricity, never showing any frustration nor tolerating any impatience or disrespect with it on the part of his children. Although I had tended to think of his patience with her as a sign of his gentleness and care, over the years it started to look more and more like passivity and tuning out. And now it began to turn. Now as my mother spoke he would sigh, trying to exchange looks with his uncomfortable children while her talk washed over us. He became noticeably impatient with her, at times bordering on cruel, as did she in return. My mother reported being fearful of him and his newly found anger, and even told me she was afraid of what he might do. And then one day he snapped; while she was launching into her playlist of interminable stories of misfortunate strangers he turned to her and said, "Your stories don't interest me." It was true, and it was cruel. My mother looked stunned, and then cried and cried. It became a story she repeatedly told, through tears, and often in front of him and visitors. When she did, he looked off to the side and said nothing.

And then my mother, three months after her bout with COVID, became sick again. While at a conference a few hours away I received a call from Elisabeth, telling me my mother had been admitted to the emergency ward with a case of respiratory syncytial virus (RSV), a condition very dangerous for the elderly, and that in her case had turned into pneumonia. I hurried back, and with Elisabeth immediately went to the hospital, where my mother had been quarantined. There we found her muttering, delirious. Half-conscious at best, my mother kept speaking, disconnected phrases piled on top of each other, surging waves and waves of verbiage, for hours. I turned to Elisabeth and whispered, "She will die of talking." We laughed softly, felt instant but shallow remorse, and then moved on, a ritual to which we had become accustomed.

The next day, her oxygen levels continued to drop, and again we sat and watched. When she regained some level of consciousness, and hovered in and out of delirium, Elisabeth distracted her by singing tacky Dutch folk songs with her, an event which has stayed with me as a memory of love and faithfulness – my mother, her hair dishevelled and upright, night shirt alarmingly askew, eyes closed, singing along in Dutch to one of our childhood songs, whose chorus imitated a dog's barking: "wuff woof, wuff woof, wuff woof." With my mother in quarantine and apparently nearing her end, we eventually got permission for my father to visit. He wasn't initially eager, and was nervous on the trip over, wondering how it would go – her being so sick, and their relationship having become increasingly bitter. I see him still, leaning over her bed and gazing at her while she slept, muttering to herself. And then she woke up, smiled at him, and whispered, "You came." And he responded tenderly, stroking her cheek. But within minutes the established pattern reasserted itself, and she was full of recriminations at the hospital, and at him. She wanted to return to their apartment, at one point yelling, "I have my rights. I am a citizen of this country. It is a free country." We returned him, alone, to their apartment, weeping.

The next morning my mother's blood oxygen level had stabilized, and then I watched it creep back to normal. The hospital, dealing with an RSV outbreak, was eager to discharge her. It wasn't pretty. She was furious and traumatized at having been tied down in her bed at the worst of her sickness, when she repeatedly tried to take out her tubes and walk around. Still not in her right mind, she distrusted everyone, sure that her belongings were being stolen, and when approached by a smiling hijab-wearing doctor, her eyes shifted back and forth and she stepped back and began muttering about the Germans and the Jews. Uncomprehending, the doctor looked at us for clarification, and we theatrically shrugged, baffled and evasive, mumbling at our toes. Full of anxiety and making no sense, my mother informed the staff that she would not agree to be released until my brother arrived from Alberta to sign the papers that her apartment was still hers. She had her rights, and loudly worried that her place in the rest home had been sold out from under her in the past five days. The staff tried to slip an Ativan into her food to calm her, which incensed her when she saw it, and then a few hours later they decided she was fit to return home. They telephoned and told us she would be discharged within hours.

Elisabeth needed to deal with the practicalities of my mother's release; my job was to tell my father about it. My father and I sat face to face, knee to knee, in his darkened living room. I looked at him and said, "Dad, uh, well, Mom is pulling through. She's being released from the hospital and will be here in a few hours." He looked stunned, said two words – "Oh no" – and burst into tears. I still don't want to probe those words too deeply; it is both clear and unclear what they meant. He loved her, but he couldn't face living with her. He wasn't so much sad as despairing. The thought of her return (and not, I uncertainly hoped, her survival) devastated him. We whisked my father away to Elisabeth's home that afternoon, and my mother returned to an empty apartment, where the first night she wandered the halls, knocking on doors trying to find my father. And that same night I flew back, through the darkness, four and a half thousand kilometres back to my home in Halifax. Nobody felt good about anything.

That is how their marriage, their parallel lives of walking though the ashes of Amersfoort, ended. He couldn't live with her anymore, and so we separated them, moving my mother into nursing care, in a separate building. It was a necessary but awful dispersal, after seventy-two years: she needed care, and he needed respite. My mother, increasingly suspicious as to why she was in the nursing ward and realizing she and my father had drifted apart, began negotiating her return. At times she would insist that she and my father both still believed they could be happy together; at other times she tried to negotiate a way to divide their apartment so they wouldn't see each other much, with her bedroom functioning as her sitting room, and she receiving kitchen privileges. And at times she would say something none of us could ever imagine her saying or that it might be true: "I don't think he loves me anymore." My father visited, but her gloom and complaints exhausted him, and because of that, triggered flashbacks to Amersfoort. He would return from his visits devastated, telling me difficult things about my mother and seeking affirmation and solidarity in a way that made me uncomfortable. At times, he would lower his voice if others were around, and tell me a small joke he had made at her expense. I found this both upsetting and disorienting – such behaviour was unimaginable in the man I knew. I would try to redirect him by referring to their many good years together and call up a memory of a happy camping trip, or some hilarious escapade my mother had engineered. Perhaps knowing what I was up to, at one point he cut me off, something he never did, and curtly said, "That was the past." Immersed in the misery of his present (which kept him locked in the distant past of the War), he was no longer interested in their intervening years together, when the two of them made a life for themselves.

And that is where he ended. While he was still capable of small joys, he was bone-tired, resolutely labouring through each day, visiting my mother every other day, bringing her a muffin and some cheese, as some kind of expression of commitment and complicated love.

Return to Amersfoort

IN THE 1980S or late 1970s my father, on one of his infrequent trips to the Netherlands, returned to Amersfoort for the first and only time since 1945. He was visiting his sister at the time and was driven there by his brother-in-law, his sister having refused to accompany him. All I have from this visit is the memory of a photograph of him, fronting the camera at a bit of a diagonal, wearing a trench coat with the wide lapels of the day. His expression is hard to read. Defiant? Barely keeping it together? Trying to look brave? I don't know, but he did want a record of it, and the record has been lost.

I have been there twice. The first time was on my second-ever trip to the Netherlands (the first was when I was sixteen), as an adult, attending an academic conference in the summer of 1997. I used the opportunity to reconnect with family, and stayed with my father's youngest brother, his only living sibling (the baby brother from his letter home). As a gracious host, Oom Martin asked me one day what I would like to do. I told him I would like to visit Amersfoort, an hour away by car – a decent-sized trip for such a small country, but not crazy. Oom Martin stopped, stunned: "Why would you want to do that?" He had never been, never wanted to, never been curious. His parents, he said, had never discussed Amersfoort; Oma always shut down any talk of it. But he agreed, and off we drove. We did not call ahead. When we arrived everything was closed. The memorial was not much developed at the time, and we just saw, from outside, a fence, the bell tower that called prisoners to appel, and what I assumed was the appel ground. This was not the trip I had anticipated. I had wanted something big, conclusive, but as we wandered, without a map, it all felt anticlimactic, flat. We ended by walking down a sandy, tree-lined path down to the execution grounds, nestled in a basin that had been dug out by prisoners more than fifty years ago, and stopped in front of Amersfoort's memorial statue of a hollow-eyed prisoner waiting to be executed, clothes hanging off him as if he were a clothes rack, coat open (in a note on the back of a photograph my father took of the statue he wrote that condemned prisoners were ordered to open their coats so that there would be minimal damage and blood spilled on them, so they could more easily be used again for the next incoming prisoner). We read the inscription, looked again, and walked back to where we had parked. We did not say much, folded ourselves back into the tiny car, and drove home in silence. When we got home Oom Martin told me he had developed a migraine. He went to his bedroom, shut the door, and I did not see him again until the next morning.

The second time was about ten years later, on a European vacation with Susan and our two children, my son the age my father was when he entered Amersfoort. A cousin and his wife drove us there, along with their children. They had never been, and his parents had never talked about what had happened to their uncle during the War. They were curious. This time Amersfoort was open and well-developed, the air completely still, the grounds silent. We toured everything, including the museum. I kept myself calm, but mainly I was watching myself keeping myself calm, including as I looked

Frits Siege, *de Stenen Man*

("Prisoner in front of the firing squad"), 1953

at the appel ground (its preserved bell now silent), where my father stood and witnessed someone being kicked to death, and where he stood, naked, on a rainy winter evening, waiting to be transported to what he thought would be his death; and at a remembrance of the rose garden, where this time there were real roses growing through barbed wire; and at the rifle range, where I thought of the prisoners who had walked and sung their way to their deaths. Over the intervening decades the rifle range had become a peaceful place, a grotto of sorts, quiet and surrounded by lovely trees whose leaves whispered in the wind. When we walked back into the camp from the execution grounds, my children, overcome by the physical presence of where their grandfather had been brutalized, reached out and the four of us hugged each other and held our embrace for a long time, slowly rocking, comforting each other next to the rose garden. My cousin stepped away for a moment, perhaps to give us some private space, and then returned to present me with a book about Kamp Amersfoort he had just bought. Holding it in my hands and looking at it, I fell into a hole, and for the first time in my life I completely lost it over Amersfoort, dropping the book and explosively weeping myself into the arms of my baffled, straight-backed cousin. Convulsive howling, nothing stifled, mucus flying everywhere. And then I just stopped. I had no idea what had just happened. The kind staff, who clearly had seen this kind of thing before, led us into a separate room to collect ourselves. They gave us coffee, and we sat for a while, while the familiar fatigue and flatness washed over me. Then we piled into my cousin's car and drove back in silence.

I don't know what these visits are supposed to be like for the second generation of camp survivors. In memoirs I have read, and according to my generic sense of what returns should be like, aged former prisoners return to visit the site of their trauma, pointing out details while they quietly talk to their children and grandchildren. Not exactly a calm time, but an emotionally important time in which things get said, before, during, and after, between parent and child. Some temporary closure, inadequate, but as much as could be expected. My second visit to Amersfoort didn't follow the genre, exactly. My father wasn't there, of course, so the quiet talk didn't materialize. As for the emotional resonance of the visit, I felt sympathy and sorrow for my father, but my dominant emotions were anger and frustration, anger and frustration at Amersfoort, at this place. It was anger for what it had done to my father, but also for what it had done to me. This is the place where everything fell apart, where possibilities constricted and boundaries drew in; this is the place from where something from before I was born, malevolent, formless and heavy, reached out across time and an ocean and grabbed me by the ankle, an unyielding, clinging grip, knocking me off balance, pulling me down, again and again. This place is what I will always drag around, the thing I will never shake off.

*

True to form, I didn't immediately tell my father I had visited Amersfoort, unable to deal with his reaction, scared that he would break down and that I would then have caused him additional suffering. And if not, if he were pleased? Did I really have the energy to open up that complication? I thought I might tell him a few years down the road, which I did, in a brief reference, but I don't remember much of his reaction, other than that he was a little startled, and didn't pursue it.

A bit disproportionate, my reaction to that Amersfoort visit, given that I have turned out basically okay. My life, after some wobbly years in early adolescence, has become more than I could have imagined. Recently retired, I was a good teacher, and students have reported on my being kind and encouraging. My scholarship made a mild difference in one corner of modernist literary studies; a few people – including young people – still refer to it. I married out of my league, but despite that, Susan – intelligent, beautiful, talented – loves and understands me, despite my sharp edges, Amersfoort-created or otherwise. My children are doing well, making a difference in their own corners of the world, with partners that seem a perfect fit. And, just recently, a beautiful grandson. I can show you pictures.

My life is good. But still, lurking in the background, at other times stepping forward and then retreating but never disappearing, is a feeling of constriction. Belatedly, I have found my own story's boundaries shaped by something that happened years before I was born, creating a mild narcissism about my identity peculiar to the second generation of camp survivors, perhaps naïvely trying to understand who they are in themselves, set apart from their parents and family, but finding much of who they are, and the contours of their story, predetermined by an unimaginable malevolence. And I have wondered how long Amersfoort's reach has been, what my children have carried away from Amersfoort, from seeing their grandfather's physical and mental slide downhill, from that long family embrace near the rose garden, and their years of watching me. My son, Benjamin, an over-thinker like his father, recently wrote me about what he sees as his Amersfoort inheritance: "a bit of extra jumpiness, a desire for privacy, an impulse to minimize risk in small ways, a strong distaste for violence, a discomfort with authority." But, he goes on, "if you think about it too hard you wind up not knowing who you are without it, and it feels really annoying to let dead Nazis have that much power."

It is annoying, and, moreover, setting the difficulties of my life next to my father's has overtones of relativizing. How can one have the self-absorption to complicate the horrors of a prison camp by setting it in the context of the anxieties of a pensioned professor, safely writing in the study of his comfortable home, a dog sleeping at his feet, a cup of excellent coffee right at hand? But to ignore the War's effect on me doesn't work either; as my mother would say, and with the same disproportion that can feel like a startling lack of empathy, "I have my own trauma." There is no balance here. Amersfoort has left its mark on me, pressing me down with anxiety about uncertainty and the fragility of things – I was always already prepared for both personal tragedy and the global horrors of climate change and the resurgence of fascism. While many people with fathers who did not live through the War also have these worries, suggesting my anxieties do not solely originate from Amersfoort in the winter of 1945, the extremity of their presence in me and the congruence of these traits with my father's trauma and how it was expressed, give me pause. I know that correlation is not causation, but it makes me suspicious.

More indelible is a mark left on me as a child, instilled by a sister's reprimand, by a mother's solemn and brusque gesture during devotions, by looking away from a father's crying. My most profound anxieties arise from uncertainty and silence, anxieties that come from reaching for things that don't acknowledge me, that silently turn away, eyes averted. Often the effect is disproportionate to the cause – fuming for hours about an email not promptly returned, or the details of an appointment not settled until the last moment, or someone forgetting to show up for a meeting. Trivial things, but an occasion for me to overreact, furious and panicky because something is out of reach and uninterpretable. At times the occasion is more semiotically weighty. My most traumatic nightmare, recurring every year or so, is of Susan leaving me, and when I reach out to find out why (I never know why, which may be another issue, I suppose), she refuses to speak, or to even come to the door. The door closes and I have to walk away without her. Her leaving me is awful, but her refusal to speak or even look at me as I continue to press is the thing that wakes me, sweating, my heart pounding and my breathing rapid and shallow. I am back in my familiar place. I am not sure what kind of comfort I get from thinking that these aspects of my personality derive from the winter of 1945. I can line all these things up and blame them on the downward sifting of Amersfoort's ashes, but the purpose and consequences of doing so are unclear. As my mother would say, "What is the use?" I am who I am.

Pressing

ONE MIGHT THINK that, looked at in a measured way about what I know and what I don't know, I have wasted many opportunities during my life with my father. Other than in the last months of his life, and then only tentatively, I never pressed to ask details of his time at Amersfoort, details which are now lost forever. Not a promising trait in a memoirist. I tended to sit, and watch. I didn't press because I was exhausted by his suffering, and there were other new issues to deal with, such as my mother's state and his relationship to her, both of my parents' health, and their greater and lesser brushes with their oncoming deaths. With all these other things going on, new crises that needed addressing, there was not enough time in a short visit to probe, to get resolution on a question about the past, whether someone had indeed been shot for stealing a potato. And maybe near my father's end I didn't press when I might have because I had had no practice in doing it, an unsatisfactory silence being the family norm. Questioning about Amersfoort had been squeezed out of my nature; there had never been a safe way to get behind the family silence, and I cannot claim anything more than an average courage. Asking my father about Amersfoort was not like requesting a book at Special Collections.

In my evasions I have not come out squeaky clean; I have at times suspected that, with all the turbulence that

Amersfoort each time set in motion, I wasn't up to knowing him any better, that I could live with the level of intimacy we had achieved. But I am not unusual in my hesitations. As the generation of World War II camp survivors dies, the witnesses that are left are increasingly second-generation people like me, with their own secondhand trauma, writing memoirs of parents or grandparents. They search archives, visit significant locations, engage translators. But at some point they all need to press into the memories of others, a father, mother, grandparent. And in doing so they tend to have the same unsettling push and pull: wanting to know, but at times when they could have gone further, they do not press to discover or confront or reconcile. This is particularly true for memoirists whose family's way of dealing with the War has been through silence and repression. For example, in *The Pendulum: A Granddaughter's Search for Her Family's Forbidden Nazi Past*, Julie Lindahl's memoir of her grandfather's Nazi past in Poland and flight to South America, Lindahl relentlessly pursues her family's past through war documents, property records, archives, and travel, enlisting multiple translators, assistants, and guides in her search. Nothing seems to stand in her way, including the disapproval of her family. But ultimately her project requires searching not just archives, but the memories of specific people, beginning with her grandmother, and her grandmother's evasive shutting down and defensiveness when the past is spoken of; to some of the survivors her grandfather terrorized in Poland, whose tracking down was an act of tenacity and some danger; to Nazi sympathizers she would encounter in her travels; and finally, to an uncle in South America, who had disappeared for years. And then, in all these encounters, at some point she stops. She stops asking and pushing, leaving unasked and unanswered questions whose answers would round out her narrative, or result in something cathartic for both her and her readers. But she doesn't, and her book ends on a lovely unresolved cadence.[17]

Lovely but odd – a writer choosing not to pursue her material, material that could make for a fuller, a more gripping and clearly motivated story. But the oddity is part of the genre. As my friend Caroline Krzakowski has pointed out to me, working on her own memoir of her family during the War, in writing about family trauma memoirists are not investigative journalists; their subject is also their family. My writing is not just about extracting information: it is shaped by an ethical choice to press or not press someone I love. With my father there was a social contract, though implicit and hazy, that I tried to follow. Caroline describes her relatives speaking about their traumatic past in short bursts, quietly, for fear of "rousing the sadness." Words about family trauma aren't just referents; they *do* things, they enter into and are part of a social context. So not pressing is complex; it is an implicitly understood gap which writers agree to hold, a gap kept in place out of concern for keeping a bond and not disrupting it. Agreeing to be hobbled by my context did not feel courageous, but it did feel right; silence can also be empathetic. And so I stuttered along.

*

A month after my father's ninety-fifth birthday I again made the trip across Canada to visit my parents – my mother in her own room in nursing, and my father in the apartment he had shared with my mother for the last ten years. It wasn't going to be an ordinary visit. I had come to help him move. The money had run out, and he was being moved into a smaller, publicly funded apartment in the same building. The move would be a time of constriction. My mother was already no longer a part of his daily routine, and his moving to a smaller apartment meant he had to rid himself of many of their shared possessions and furniture. In preparation he had been curiously okay with that, occasionally telling Elisabeth of this or that item, "I don't want it here."

When I arrived with my daughter, Annelies, for the visit, my father had been sick for a few days, and his apartment was under quarantine. Masks, gowns, gloves were required, meals were brought in, and he was not allowed out. Fully covered, we entered a silent apartment, under some disarray with the preliminaries of a move – half-filled boxes, tables loaded with papers, drawers half-empty. My father was asleep, so Annelies and I set to work, careful to limit our noise. After a while we heard him stir, and went in to help him wake – quietly, so as not to startle him and trigger a panic attack. He was too weak to sit up on his own, so we each took a side and an elbow and helped him sit up, while he wept and tried to collect himself. He was like a fragile boy waking from a nap. We held him up for a long while, sitting pressed against him, and spoke slowly and clearly. He had become very deaf, and his eyes were now a watery blue, his voice gravelly. After a while we needed to return to work, having just thirty-six hours to complete the move. A few hours later we got his bed downstairs, made it up, and brought him down to sleep. We helped him on to his bed, and with tears streaming down his face he cried, saying over and over, "I am so tired, I am so tired." And then he slept, completely still, for a few hours.

I had spent the previous weeks thinking about whether to tell my father of my writing about our life together. My worries were multiple: would he cry, would it bring his trauma to the surface, would it be unhelpful for him? I wondered about my own motivations for telling him, whether it was to give him some closure or peace, or to scavenge material for my book. And I had pragmatic hesitations, about what his expectations about the book might be, and what to do if he were opposed to my writing about him at all. Elisabeth said she thought knowing about my project would make him happy, so I decided, against my cultivated instincts and fears, to press on. Initially, my telling him didn't seem to register, but two days later he was more responsive. And so, at his ninety-five and my sixty-three, my father and I had our first-ever extended conversation about Amersfoort. In his new apartment, darker and more constricted than his previous one, with most of the remaining items of his life still waiting to be put in their new places, the pendulum wall clock he had inherited from his parents lying on its side, its weights trailing on the ground and its loud ticking quiet for the time being, he began to talk.

We sat down and had some tea together. I told him of the research I had been doing, and that I had seen his Amersfoort documents (he was baffled that they existed), that my inquiries had revealed that there had been more killing at Amersfoort than at any other place in the Netherlands, that his own story of being returned to Amersfoort for a week filled in a gap for the memorial staff there, and that I would like to get access to his Red Cross documents. In turn, punctuated by short moments of soft crying, he told me something of his time in Amersfoort, familiar ground initially, and then something new, of being beaten for carrying wood improperly on his return from his work detail, he having shifted the load because of how it bore down on his prominent clavicle. Then, for the first time he referred not just generally to "the guards," but mentioned his tormentors by name. "I have seen Kotälla in action," he told me. "Kotälla was the devil himself." It did not surprise him to learn what I had discovered, that even the Nazis had decided Kotälla needed to go on leave for a while, to get serious psychiatric treatment before he could return to his duties.

Then my father turned to his life after the War, telling me to check the postmark on his letter home from Amersfoort – a letter his eyes had been unable to read for a decade or more – that the date was March 17, a month after he arrived home. He then described his loneliness on his return to Loosduinen, with nobody willing to talk about what had happened to him. In a rare burst of sarcasm, he mentioned the minister of his church, who told him, "'Oh yeah, I will talk to you.' Well, he still has to." More than his treatment in Amersfoort, it seemed that near the end of his life he was most unsettled, even bitter, about his community and family's refusal to engage with his trauma, of sending him off and keeping him on a long road of isolated silence.

It was not a long conversation, perhaps fifteen minutes. He agreed that I could send his letter home to the archives at Amersfoort, and that we could put up his photograph on their memorial wall. And with his now-indecipherable penmanship he signed papers allowing me to look up his records in the National Archives in The Hague. He was happy that I was writing his story, and thanked me. Did he believe it would only be about him as a sufferer, or as a hero? I don't think so, but I don't know. He was happy that someone was doing some work, that someone was paying attention. And he knew the purpose of my questions, that they weren't mainly about helping him to work through things; they were to get information. It was an amazing moment, but he did not take the War up again when I saw him the next day, even when I gave him an opening to do so. The day after that, Annelies and I flew back to Halifax, folding our bodies into the cramped seats at the back of the economy cabin for the long trip home.

Memory, Again

THIS IS WHAT memory looks like, sometimes.

Five months before my father died Susan and I flew out west to see my parents. Our daily visits to my father on this trip were short, his exhaustion weighing heavily on him, his voice barely able to rise above a whisper. When Susan and I arrived at his apartment one day, his door was locked. We knocked, and after a bit of a wait he came to the door, opened it, then turned around and silently led us to his living area. He did not attempt his weak but cheery hello that morning. He slowly eased himself into his chair, put one hand over his eyes, and began to cry, softly at first, but with increasing intensity, until his breathing became more and more ragged and gasping; his tremor turned into noticeable shaking, causing his arms to wave uncontrollably; and then his whole body began to convulse. He managed to gasp out a request for his Ativan. Susan brought it to him and then slowly, slowly, he steadied, roused himself a bit, looked sheepishly up, and apologized for what he called his Hitler shakes. He told us he had had a flashback.

Within minutes he was overcome again. Looking directly at Susan, who was sitting closely in front of him, he began an explosive recounting of his most painful memories of the War: of standing naked in the winter cold, of his one week without food, of dysentery and the eyes of his fellow prisoner, of three men defiantly singing as they were led to their deaths, of the man kicked to death, of holding up his fellow prisoner during appel, of the bombing and panic in Gronau. It was his canon of trauma memories, each one brief and disconnected from the others, in no particular order, in images and flashes rather than as narratives, an explosive vomiting out of memories. As the speed increased, we disappeared from his consciousness, and he descended into disconnected words and groaning, guttural and animalistic. He had become something else; he had become his memories, his trauma a carapace squeezing him tighter and tighter. In the middle of it I thought I heard him calling to God.

And then, slowly calming once more, he returned to the world and began to speak about the bitterness of being lonely after the War, and then about not hating. As he disengaged from what had possessed him, we eventually all shifted and began to talk, together, about other memories, of hilarity and contentment, of family camping trips, of dinner-time kerfuffles.

Susan and I left him sitting in his chair, everyone exhausted. The indignity of what we witnessed, of my father's past assaulting his entire being, taking his dignity and autonomy and grinding them into the ground, was grotesque. Not just the physical assault, but the exponential disproportion of it left me, and still leaves me, stunned. What right had those five weeks in the winter of 1945 to relentlessly stalk and brutalize him – even, violently, down to his last days? And I was baffled about what his frantic recounting of his memories accomplished, what did this *do*? Susan, to whom he had never spoken about Amersfoort, who had never seen *this* before (was he doing it for her, finally telling her?), pointed out that it was a different experience from someone sharing painful memories with you. It wasn't a retelling. It wasn't a recounting or a request for empathy as much as he was *living* it, again. It was exhausting to be in the presence of this, and I just hung on, eyes wide open this time, looking at him, and I waited it out, leaning forward and stroking his arm.

Waiting

AFTER A WHILE with the very old who have suffered for years and whose bodies are tired, you realize something has changed: you are waiting for the end. Not desiring it, but waiting for it. You watch the person you have loved your whole life as one by one things get closed off; it becomes too difficult to get in the car, walks get shorter and shorter, eyes can't handle jigsaw puzzles or watch television anymore, ears have to strain too hard to hear music, and the mind can't concentrate on audiobooks. There are moments of great tenderness and meaning, but in the waiting there are few events and it is clear that the end is near, and you both know it. It feels something like waiting to leave for the airport after a visit, the flight having been delayed a few hours, but the suitcases have been packed, and there is nothing to do but sit in the living room and occasionally break the silences by repeating a few of the old stories, telling a few of the jokes, and maybe sometimes surprising each other with something. The last couple of years of my father's life were like that, as he became weaker and weaker, more and more exhausted. A few moments stand out for me, emblematic of who he was, of who he wanted to be, of how I think he wanted things to end.

*

When it was clear that my parents could no longer live together should my mother return from the hospital, my brother took my father to look at a small publicly funded apartment in the home, publicly funded for when the money would run out, as it eventually would. Each parent would have their own small place. We were worried how he would react, this being such a step down from what he had been living in, a two-bedroom unit with a large living room with many windows and a view. Leaning on his walker, my father stood in the doorway, peered in silently, and then turned to my brother, saying: "I have spent time in solitary confinement – this doesn't look so small to me."

*

My father told me, on the day my mother turned ninety-nine, that he was finished talking with his counsellor. He said there was nothing more to go over with her about either my mother or Amersfoort. But around a week or two later he had one last occasion on which he spoke about the War. At ninety-five, my father decided to attend the Men's Club in his rest home. Oddly, it was his first time. At each meeting a resident would present a topic for discussion. This day the speaker decided to read a chapter from a book about the War. My father reported that it was excellent and beautiful writing. But as the reading progressed he found himself immersed in and reliving his own time in the War, back in Amersfoort, in the winter, standing at attention in appel, starving, in the cold. He knew he should leave, but his pathological politeness and sense of obligation held him in his seat. It would be rude to leave and to interrupt the moment others were having. So he sat through the whole thing, falling deeper and deeper into the past. At the end there was time for discussion, and as members of the audience began to comment on what they had heard, my father interrupted, standing himself up to say, "I know all about this. I was sixteen years old and I was in a concentration camp. Sorry folks, but I have to leave." And then he reached for his walker and left. It was his briefest telling of his time at Amersfoort, given as an apology, an apology in both senses – as an expression of regret and as a defense, much milder and both like and unlike the times he had apologized to me. The story was simple: a boy of sixteen was imprisoned and degraded by the Nazis, and some eighty years later he still was defined by it. My father was announcing his limits, and there was a tinge of genteel defiance in what he did, a physical and emotional leave-taking that was both flight and fight, drawing a line between hearing about history and personally living with its trauma.

*

And then, in the last year of his life my father did something startling. He asked to bless me, by which he meant something formal, in the biblical way of Isaac blessing Jacob, and Jacob blessing Joseph's sons. Patriarchal blessings in the book of Genesis point to the future, extending God's blessings to a world which the older man will not see. The idea made me uncomfortable, but he was my father, and he was old. And so he did it, in his own way, in the quiet of his apartment, an apartment without my mother, putting his shaking hands on my shoulders while I knelt in front of him, my hands on his knees, just as he wished. This time he did not cry. His blessing wasn't quite within the genre, not so much about the future.

He wasn't thinking about the future; he was thinking about his past and offered a prayer of thanks for parts of it: for me, for my life, for the time we were given to be with each other. He thanked God for the care and protection he had given us. After he was done, I stepped into the occasion and responded with a blessing of my own to him, one that didn't live up to the complexities of living with him, but that was true nonetheless, giving thanks for my father and the privilege it had been to be his son. Neither of us acknowledged this, but the blessings were a way of addressing his impending death. When we were done we both cried in the family way, each looking off to the side. Then I stood up, feeling a bit of my own age in my knees, and we had coffee together, and talked about other things.

*

Afterword

TWO MONTHS SHY of her hundredth birthday, my mother talked to me of how she saw her role in dealing with my father's War, of her matter-of-fact turning away from the trauma, of holding the lid down and getting on with things. This was the first time she had spoken to me of this. Over the course of a few days she repeatedly returned to this topic, mulling over whether she had been an unduly hard mother, or whether it might be more accurate to think of herself as strong. Her speculation weighed on her; she knew that over the years her children thought her actions showed that she lacked empathy for my father's suffering. But she told me that in the aftermath of Amersfoort she had needed to be strong. She had protected us, and the vindication of her strategy was that we had turned out alright. And so she eventually settled, with retrospective satisfaction, and maybe a little too much emphasis, on what she saw as her positive legacy, the thing that helped us turn out alright: "I kept the War from you kids."

*

My father was the reason for my visit. A few weeks earlier he had fallen and broken his femur, leading, as it does for the extremely aged, to an inevitable downhill slide. And so I had flown out on what would be my last crisis trip for him. Unlike earlier trips to my parents, this time there would be no turning back from death; his trajectory became more and more clear over the length of my stay. He became increasingly delirious over the days of my visit, at times ripping off his hospital gown and covers, trying to get out of bed and go home, while I struggled to hold him in his bed and cover his nakedness, my eyes averted. And then one day, my sister and I having secured a place for him in hospice care, I had to fly back home. On my way to the airport I had a final stop to see him, my ride waiting outside the main door in the hospital turnaround. I entered quietly, pushed aside the beige curtain that separated his bed from the others, and found my father asleep, his breathing occasionally stuttering but deep. I tried but could not wake him without the danger of startling him and awakening the Amersfoort within, and as a result he slept until the very end of my visit, at which point, as I was putting on my coat to leave, he woke up, his pale blue eyes fluttering. I leaned over him: "Dad, it's Len. I've come to say goodbye. I have to go back home now. I love you." He had difficulty speaking, but in between deep breaths, he managed a few short phrases. "Thanks for coming," he said, as he always did. As I sat next to him, holding his hand and weeping, he said, "It's alright." After another pause, heavy, he gathered his breath and said, "I love you" and "God bless you." He then went back into his silence. And then I, having received his final gift, had to leave for my afternoon flight, back to Halifax, flying east, but into the dark. He died eight days later.

*

About two weeks after his death I was back in British Columbia for his funeral and to help with my father's effects, deciding on what needed to be kept, and what could be discarded. There was not a lot to do. He had spent his last months going through photos, documents, and belongings, pruning and organizing them so that his children would not have too much work when he passed. He did not get rid of everything, particularly items related to the War: newspapers, flyers, and comics from the time of the liberation; my mother's multiple letters that eventually gave my father and our family financial restitution for his suffering, odd and inadequate trade-off though it was; his own letter home from Amersfoort; and the letter from his father. Some of these items had prefatory notes that he had typed up some time after coming to Canada. I found the map he had drawn of Amersfoort as he remembered it, drawn for his book back in the late 1980s, his drawing and penmanship, always having been precise, here starting to show signs of his tremor. A small, curated collection, containing items I was familiar with.

Among these materials I also found two things I had never seen before. The first was a copy of his book, in almost pristine shape, the book he had written as an apologia to his children and grandchildren. I opened it up to find a different addressee, in his inscription, in Dutch:

> To Mother
> From Nell and Dick
> July/91

Nothing more, just this bare address to his mother, who died a little more than a year later. My guess is that this copy found its way back to my father after Oma's death, sent by one of his siblings, having found it among her personal effects.

Less clear is what the gift of this book might have meant to my father and to Oma. It seemed by its bareness to be enveloped in silence. What kind of gesture was this on my father's part? And how was it received? Was it a peace offering, or a reprimand? Did they both see it in the same way? What did Oma make of the bare inscription, which, being in Dutch, contained the only words she was able to read? I have no idea what she thought of this book, whether she it saw as something that needed a response, or as something just to put away on her shelf.

And then, a second item: three double-sided typed pages in italic font, held together by a paper clip that had left a rusty stain on the front and back pages. They were notes from my father's first round of counselling in the mid-1980s, almost forty years before his death, when he was fifty-seven years old. Rough transcriptions of six sessions, they appeared to have been typed up from notes made by his therapist during the course of those sessions, with my father having done some mild follow-up corrections in black pen. One last document from a man's life. As with the documents I had received from Amersfoort, initially I frantically gulped them down, and then settled myself and went over them again more slowly, noting my father's return to several themes and images, and an odd phrase, standing out by itself: "What bothers me most now is the lopsidedness."

And then I sat, silent once again, for a half hour, staring out my front window but not focusing. It was my father, in his first session with his counsellor, talking about the War again, this time not as a man testifying to God's protection, but as a person at the end of his rope, a person in profound struggle, speaking of his self-doubts and humiliations, reaching for help, wanting to be heard, this time:

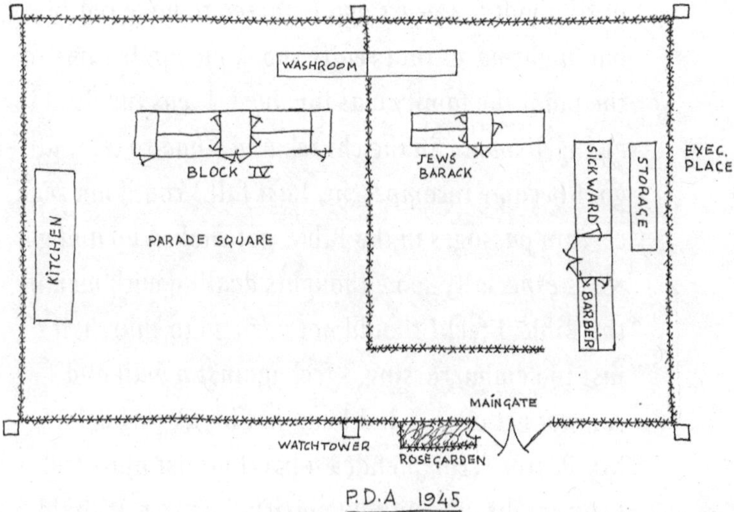

Dirk Diepeveen, schematic rendering of Kamp Amersfoort, ca. 1990

I was incarcerated in a concentration camp at the age of 16 and I escaped spent three months in hiding with my grandparents. I tried to forget about it. I wanted to talk but there was nobody to talk to. I worked hard and thought everything was fine until about ten years ago I started to have really bad nightmares that really shook me up. It came to the point the family was involved, I was involved in evangelism etc. in the church and I had to let it all go. I became incompetent. Last fall I could not read certain passages in the Bible, got choked up and got tears especially some thoughts dealing with men in the Bible. I feel I should not even go to church, it's just too embarrassing. I feel against a wall and I can not get over it and I can not break through it. My Pastor recommended a psychiatrist but I feel I cannot discuss without spiritual aspect. It could be my immigration to Canada, a flight from bad memories. It took a lot of power just to make the phone call to the counselling centre I am scared. In my family things were never talked about among my parents but I have a Father in heaven Who looks after things. There's no way for me to talk. My father had arthritis and suffered. My mother was in control and we could not talk about personal things. I don't have any bitterness. A Nazi after the war became my best friend. A German made mine fields and we dug them up and then the farmer was able to put his corn back in. There were about six friends and they kept chasing us. The Germans kept chasing the six of us. We stumbled over a deserted Dutch soldier and there were lots of weapons. A friend of mine who was a youth leader got killed and was executed. Mom and I decided to go to my grandparents. My father was away, and so I was the oldest in the family. I was put in a police cell and I had a personal I.D. card that was falsified and a friend of mine in the underground did it. But I said I had done it. I was put in a group with the Jews where there was violent treatment. We were hit over the head etc. We got sick and very very cold. I froze my hands and my feet. We were put in a rose garden between barbed wire fences. We suffered a lot of verbal abuse. Then there was a roll call and if you were missing they would search and if they found you they would torture you. The Red Cross would bring us food. We stayed there five weeks. During the night weak people were shot. You never knew if you would be alive the next day. I wasn't scared and all there were in the camp were Christians and communists. But there were stool pigeons so we could not talk freely. In February 1945, the allied forces came close. We were transported to Germany and I was sick with dysentery. I got on the train and the friends tried to escape and many of them got shot. I was ready to jump off then I saw people killed, back on to placed in a school.

> *In Germany there were sicker and sicker people and finally death. I was put in a hospital and there I escaped with the help of the medical staff. Again false papers and I went to my grandparents. During the train ride we were taken prisoners again. We escaped again, had a two hour walk and I had my clothes with me. Mother was there for the reunion. I wanted to get it off my chest. My grandparents did not understand and I couldn't talk to my mother they wouldn't listen. I had a letter from my Dad when I came back and he said, "When I come back we will talk." But it never happened. He could not face the pain. Then I came back and the friend that had falsified my papers made funny remarks about my shaved head. I had covered for him and he gave me such an ugly reception. Boy I'm surprised at how much I have shared. Last Saturday and Sunday I had terrible nightmares. I broke down and my wife broke down. And then we decided that something has to be done. It affects my work and my concentration. Now I am starting to think about it during the day.*

*

My earliest memory of my father crying, perhaps my first memory of him, was when I was four years old. We are sitting at the kitchen table at the end of dinner, me next to my mother, my father at the head of the table, about to pray. And then he suddenly breaks down weeping, not with stifled sobs, but loudly and convulsively, his bowed head in his hands, a man unprotected. It is November 22, 1963, and John Kennedy has been shot. I return to this memory every once in a while, thinking about its hold in my mind, trying to understand what it might mean. This time, at this table and on this day, my father was crying for someone else, I think. But was it perhaps also for himself, for the end of a hope that he had left all that behind, left it across the ocean and long ago, but here it was, in front of him, a malevolent violence that could take away hope and a new world whenever it wanted? Or was he crying for the whole world? I don't know. What I do know is that around the time of his convulsive crying I began to wet the bed.

Watching him for decades I know that certain kinds of hope were not available to him. I think that for my father, after the great cruelty and trauma that was incised into his body, the body of a sixteen-year-old boy, a redemptive arc was impossible. Some things are permanently broken. But they can be beautiful nonetheless, if you watch closely. In Arthur Miller's *Death of a Salesman*, another work I regularly turned to while teaching, there is a moment when Linda, the wife of Willy Loman, a man who has been relentlessly ground down by the world, turns to her uncomprehending sons to reset their focus on what is happening in front of them, to their father:

> I don't say he's a great man. Willy Loman never made a lot of money. His name was never in the paper. He's not the finest character that ever lived. But he's a human being, and a terrible thing is happening to him. So attention must be paid. He's not to be allowed to fall into his grave like an old dog. Attention, attention must be finally paid to such a person.[18]

It is a moment in the play that I always have found a little stagey, perhaps overdone, requiring a little too much pause in the action and stress in the voice – too great a shift from the staccato sound and conflict that surrounds it. A separate moment of analysis, it is almost a set piece, difficult to pull off for an actor because of that sudden shift. But maybe, just because of that, it is a brilliant piece of realism. Sometimes, having closely watched someone for a long time, we realize something important has happened and we raise our voice, modulate into a higher key, because the occasion, the person deserves it. And if others find the voice a little corny, the rhetoric a little high, the tremble unwarranted, that is just the cost of being human.

My father and I shared a life not so much of big dramatic encounters, but instead of small moments of grace, muddled though they were. We evaded and came to each other at a slant, slightly and always askew, but beautiful, beautiful for all of that and because all of that. In a difficult time, as darkness descends again, and new ash begins to settle down around us and we breathe it in, we need to pay attention.

Notes

1 Harry Mulisch, *The Assault*, translated by Claire Nicolas White (New York: Pantheon Books, 1985), 55.

2 Marcel Proust, *Remembrance of Things Past*, translated by C.K. Scott Moncrieff (New York: Random House, 1934).

3 G. Von Frijtag Drabbe Künzel, *Kamp Amersfoort* (Amsterdam: Mets & Schilt, 2003), 182.

4 *Kamp Amersfoort*, 200–01.

5 *Kamp Amersfoort*, 163.

6 Daniel Mendelsohn, *The Lost: A Search for Six of Six Million* (New York: HarperCollins, 2006), 210–11.

7 Primo Levi, *The Periodic Table*, translated by Raymond Rosenthal (New York: Schocken Books, 1984), 213.

8 *The Periodic Table*, 215.

9 *The Periodic Table*, 221.

10 *The Periodic Table*, 218.

11 *The Periodic Table*, 223.

12 Colossians 3:13, Luke 6:37, Matthew 18:21. Revised Standard Version.

13 *Kamp Amersfoort*, 209–10.

14 Email communication, June 25, 2024.

15 "Ervaringen van de bemanningen der getorpedeerde loggers" [Experiences of the crews of the torpedoed luggers], *Haagsche Courant* (The Hague: 26 November 1917), retrieved through delpher.nl.

16 Email communication, November 28, 2022.

17 Julie Lindahl, *The Pendulum: A Granddaughter's Search for Her Family's Forbidden Nazi Past* (Lanham, MD: Rowman and Littlefield, 2018).

18 Arthur Miller, *Death of a Salesman*, ed. Gerald Clifford Weales (Penguin Books, 1996), 56.

Acknowledgments

There were many helping hands along the way in writing this memoir. Thanks to Aarnoud van der Spoel, Nic Chadwick, and Kenneth Harvie for help with translation from Dutch to English, and to Ray Jahncke for research on the weather in Amersfoort in 1945. The staff at Nationaal Monument Kamp Amersfoort, particularly Eddy van der Pluijm and Floris van Dijk, patiently replied to my queries. In finding out about what really happened to Opa Spaans, I am indebted to Chris Bell and Samuël Kruizinga, who pointed me in the right direction. Theo Legters and Annelies van der Hammen Legters cheerfully worked in the Dutch National Archives on my behalf and also tracked down an image of Psalm 43.

I am in debt to Bruce Greenfield, who made his way through an early version of this book and gave me the right advice about painful cuts I needed to make; to Mary Ellen Geist for her belief in the project; and to Tim van Laar – not just his support for this book but for the gift of thirty years of writing together.

Early on, professional advice helped me find my way in a publishing landscape that was new to me. A conversation with Shauntay Grant helped set me on my way, as did a talk with Stephen Kimber, who nudged me in the right direction at the right time. Patrick Crean's careful attention to the manuscript and my goals for it gave the book clearer focus. Most important for developing this memoir, a chance introduction to Caroline Krzakowski led to the most productive writing partnership I could have wanted.

And then there are those who brought this book into the world. Special thanks to my agent, Pieter Swinkels of Transatlantic Literary Agency, who has kept me steady through the whole process – a considerable task – and whose belief in and understanding of this memoir connected me with presses I am honoured to be associated with. I am grateful to Kelsey Attard of Freehand Books for taking on this project so enthusiastically, and for her support throughout the process. I could not imagine a better experience. Thanks, too, to Debbie Willis, to whose sharp eye and editorial sense I am in debt – the book is clearer for her work. For the Dutch edition, I am thankful to Querido's Patricia de Groot, Jan Willem Reitsma, and Marion Bruinenberg.

This is a book deeply embedded in my family: my three siblings, who lived through, and continue to live through, the War in their own ways. I owe especial gratitude to Elisabeth, for her care for my father, and her help in sorting out details as I wrote during the final frantic months of my father's life. And my mother, who has recently died at the age of 102: a complicated woman, who loved us and who, using what she knew and had at hand, got her children through. And closer in, my own children, Ben and Annelies, for caring for my parents over the years. And closer still, to Susan, who for more than forty years has been a generous and loving presence to my parents, and to me. Her support during the writing of this book, in both the good moments and the times when she needed me to just calm down, has been deeper than I could have imagined.

LEONARD DIEPEVEEN is the Emeritus George Munro Professor of Literature and Rhetoric at Dalhousie University. He has published widely as a scholar of modernist literature and visual art, and in 2020 was elected as a Fellow of the Royal Society of Canada. He lives in Halifax, Nova Scotia.